the white stripes

the white stripes

21st
Century
Blues

Dick Porter

Plexus, London

British Library Cataloguing in Publication Data

Porter, Dick
    The White Stripes : 21st century blues
    1. White Stripes (Group) 2. Rock musicians - United States
I. Title
782.4'2166'0922

ISBN 0 85965 350 1

Cover design by Brian Flynn
Book design by Brian Flynn
Printed in Great Britain by Bell & Bain, Glasgow

Contents

1. as if from heaven 9

2. minimum r&b 25

3. image can kill love 45

4. a bigger room 65

5. a box with something in it 93

6. them chains, they're about
   to drag me down 113

   discography 138
   acknowledgements 141

The sweetheart, the gentleman –
it's the same thing.
These ideas seem to be in decline,
and I hate it.
You look at your average teenager
with the body piercings and the tattoos.
You have white kids going around
talking in ghetto accents
because they think that makes them hard.
It's so cool to be hard.
We're against that.

Jack White

We take the stars
from the blue union from heaven,
the red from our mother country,
separating it by white stripes,
thus showing we have separated
from her, and the white stripes
shall go down to posterity
representing liberty.

George Washington

I was looking for a quote
to put in our first single
that would sum up the band,
and I swear to God I opened
an encyclopedia at the thrift store
and I opened up to the page
with that quote in it.
I couldn't believe it.

Jack White

as if from heaven

You can sing the blues in church if you use the words right. *Son House*

1

The White Stripes represent the past, present and future of rock 'n' roll. In seven years, the duo have risen from unbilled appearances at Detroit bars to headlining major festivals around the globe. The fact that much of their unique sound is derived from the blues hardly sets the duo apart as trailblazers, nor does it explain the intense critical acclaim, obsessive fan-worship and chart-topping sales figures that prompted *Mojo* to describe the pair as 'the most important band on earth today'.

In terms of the influence of blues on their music, Jack and Meg White are the contemporary end of a lineage that stretches back to the Mississippi Delta, via the adaptations of Muddy Waters, John Lee Hooker, Jimi Hendrix, Jimmy Page, and innumerable others – all of whom have adapted and advanced the form during the second half of the twentieth century. The White Stripes' raw fusion of the blues with a melange of rock, country and folk elements is firmly rooted in this tradition.

What *is* radical about the band is how the sum of their influences have been combined, with directness and intelligence, to drag the blues headfirst into the new millennium. Entirely based around Jack's distorted guitar virtuosity and 'screaming-girl' vocal gymnastics, underpinned by Meg's metronomic drum salvos, the White Stripes' hyper-amped blues/rock has left critics groping for the appropriate classification. The duo's distinctive sound was described by the UK's *Daily Mirror* as 'blunk [blues-punk] rock', whereas Jack opted for the term 'Okie [Oklahoman] rock' as a tongue-in-cheek nod to its folk roots. The huge sound produced by the duo provides a manifest contrast with the two pale, fragile figures who can be seen huddled together on stages across the globe. Since their formation in 1997, the White Stripes have become a genuine phenomenon – and the most important group of the new millennium.

Jack White came into the world on 9 July 1975, as John Anthony Gillis – the seventh son of ten children born to Gorman McKenzie Gillis and his wife Teresa. The Gillis family lived in a three-storey wooden house at 1203 Ferdinand Avenue, in the Mexicantown neighbourhood of South West Detroit. As its name implies, Mexicantown is home to Detroit's small Hispanic community and is known for its range of cheap delicatessens and restaurants.

Despite the size of their home, the family were lower middle-class rather than wealthy – the collapse of heavy industry in the area during the 1970s meant that property prices hit rock bottom. The young John Anthony, having acquired the traditional nickname

Bang bang! Jack takes aim at Meg in early 2002, close to the release of **White Blood Cells.**

'Jack', was packed off to the local Montessori school for some progressive education. The inclusion of music lessons on his school's timetable revealed the first signs of his embryonic abilities.

'There was a drum circle with all the kids passing around a little bongo drum,' explained Jack. 'I was the last person in the circle, and when it got to me I played "Shave and a Haircut, Two Bits" in front of all the parents. Blew the crowd away at five years old.' Such a musical aptitude was standard among the Gillis clan – several of his older brothers performed with local bands, which ensured Jack had ready access to a wide range of instruments. 'I just always wanted to be involved in music,' recalled Jack, 'I was so excited by it. I was the kind of kid who wanted to play at four o'clock in the morning, play the drums or something.'

On the last day of school, I would go outside and kiss the ground like the Pope does when he lands in a new country. But all the other kids didn't know about the Pope doing that so they would make fun of me. *Jack White*

By the time he was ready to enter grade school, Jack had cobbled together a rudimentary drum kit and was practising regularly. Moving to a large, multicultural school provided Jack with his first taste of alienation – his preference for the organic rock of Led Zeppelin and Cream over the prevailing hip-hop/house culture of the mid 1980s instantly cast him in the role of outsider.

'I didn't really have much of a great time in grade school, so I like writing about that,' Jack recalled. 'I write about it a lot – actually having friends in grade school and having a girlfriend or something back then when you really wanted it. Kids are just so cruel sometimes. It's nice to fantasise that they're not.'

Irrespective of this peer-group anxiety, Jack stuck to his guns. 'It would have been easy for me to give up and listen to house music and techno. At least then I would have had friends. But it just seemed odd to me for white kids to pretend to have a black accent, to pretend to be from the ghetto when they are from the suburbs.'

Although the partial cause of his schoolyard isolation, music also provided Jack with a creative outlet. Inevitably, this brought him into contact with other kids who shared his interests. 'I was joining bands as a younger teenager. I just wanted to be a part of it, at any cost,' he acknowledged. An attempt to make an early four-track recording with a schoolmate who played bass prompted Jack to switch instruments. 'I taught myself guitar just so we could record something and I started singing so we could have something to play along to.'

Jack's move from drums to guitar and vocals took him closer to the fundamentals of lyrics and melody. As he later explained, this led to a broadening of his musical horizons. 'At fourteen or fifteen I didn't really think about lyrics or anything. I was just mostly into melody. I didn't know who it was that I was hearing and then I found out, "oh, country music?" I'm from Detroit and it was hard enough to be the only person in school who liked rock 'n' roll. Let alone country music. That's probably why I didn't go out and buy it or anything.'

As Jack's palette of influences expanded, he found himself driven back towards the roots of the music. 'I was into rockabilly as a teenager. The rock 'n' roll led me to the blues because I kept trying to go further back to the people I liked and finding out what their influences were and just going further back.' Jack's discovery of the blues was his personal epiphany, 'The blues was the biggest thing that blew my mind,' he later recounted. 'I felt that I'd missed so much, and wasted so much time on useless ideas about music. I wanted to become a songwriter and express myself.'

On leaving school in 1992, Jack enrolled as a music student at the Lewis Cass Technical High School. However, he quickly became disillusioned and quit after just one semester. 'I was so upset that those kids acted exactly the same way that they did in high school. I thought there was going to be a new thing, where all of a sudden you wouldn't have to deal with that crap anymore, with peer pressure and people judging everyone. I was so upset that it was the same thing all over again. My way to deal with it was to try to relate to older people and get away from that.'

When I discovered the blues, I wanted to get super honest and super in touch with soulfulness and truth. I didn't want to overtly express that notion, because it would be superficial-sounding or egotistical. *Jack White*

Jack's escape from the childishness of his peers involved securing an apprenticeship in upholstery, which he'd begun while still in high school. Brought up as part of a Catholic family in a largely Catholic neighbourhood, Jack later claimed his mother would have liked him to train as a priest ('I almost went to the seminary'). However, Jack's natural dexterity and slightly unnerving interest in taxidermy made upholstery a more practical choice.

Muldoon Upholstery was run by Brian Muldoon, a family friend in his mid-thirties, who recalls, 'I was talking to his older brother, and asked if Jack wanted to help out – tearing stuff up, doing deliveries – so he started working in my shop.' In addition to teaching his new apprentice the rudiments of the trade, Muldoon also played a significant

Son House: 'pure emotion,' according to admirer Jack White.

part in broadening Jack's musical perspective.

'Jack didn't have a record collection then,' Muldoon revealed, 'he was into Helmet, AC/DC and, like most seventeen-year-old kids, Led Zeppelin. He became fascinated with Dick Dale, the Flat Duo Jets, the Stooges and [Detroit garage rockers] the Gories, which influenced us a lot. And [MC5 vocalist] Rob Tyner's singing was a real influence for him. That was the stuff we were playing all the time in the shop while we worked. And it wasn't long before Jack was writing his own songs.'

Muldoon's musical tutelage of his willing student led to the duo holding regular jam sessions. 'After we were done working, we'd set up in the shop and play,' recalled Jack. With Muldoon occupying the drum stool, the two upholsterers gradually established a repertoire of blues standards and original compositions, some of which would ultimately form the basis of the White Stripes' eponymous 1999 debut album.

The dual influences of master bluesmen such as Son House, Robert Johnson and Lead Belly, and the rock heritage of his hometown, provided Jack with the launch pad for his future musical direction. To the young guitarist, the authenticity and simplicity of the blues represented the essence of purity of expression.

'At that point I was like, what have I been doing? Why have I not been paying attention to this music? It was that honesty, bare bones, to the minimum, truth. The more I thought about it, it was the pinnacle of songwriting. Easily accessible because of the repeating lines you could sing along to, very easy to play for the performer, extremely emotional at the same time.'

In particular, it was Son House, and his song 'Grinning In Your Face', that made the biggest impression on Jack. 'I just thought for the first time that I had heard something real. There was nothing glamorous about it – just pure sound, pure emotion. It didn't need anything else attached to it. It didn't need five other guys playing the exact same thing behind it. Just a guy and a guitar.'

House's influence would loom large over the White Stripes' later output. Their first album was dedicated to him, and the band later covered several of the legendary blues-man's compositions, including 'Death Letter' and 'John The Revelator'. 'Whenever I discovered Son House, I just flipped out,' Jack revealed. 'I couldn't believe what I'd been missing. Something just snapped, and I said, "forget all this other stuff I've been listening to. I don't want to even think about it anymore. This is exactly what's perfect and what's beautiful about music and I want to get as close to it as possible, if I can get away with it." And the White Stripes became that.'

One of the most important 1930s blues stylists, Son House's birth certificate indicates he was born Eddie James House Jr., in Riverton, Mississippi on 21 March 1902. However, evidence suggests he may have been born as early as 1886, and adjusted his birth date so that he wouldn't be considered too old to labour on the railroad during the 1950s.

The Blues? It's the mother of American music. That's what it is – the source. B.B. King

In keeping with his deeply religious upbringing, House began preaching at the age of fifteen and became a pastor before his 21st birthday. In 1927, upon hearing a street performance by a blues guitarist named Willie Wilson, Son House experienced a similar revelatory awakening to that which would strike Jack Gillis over 60 years later. Purchasing a battered 'old piece of guitar' for $1.50, House quickly set about mastering the bottleneck assisted slide technique that was to become his trademark.

Legend has it that, no sooner had House started performing at local parties and juke joints, than he was charged with manslaughter after allegedly shooting a man in self-defence. But state records reveal that the only 'Ed House' convicted during the relevant period was a bootlegger sentenced to the Parchman Penal Work Farm (later immortalised in the blues standard 'Parchment Farm') for illegally manufacturing liquor.

On his release from prison Son House resumed his musical career, touring widely with other notable blues players such as Charley Patton and Willie Brown. Although he made a number of recordings during the 1930s and forties, House was badly exploited (receiving nothing more than a bottle of Coca Cola for his original recording of 'Death Letter') and by 1948 had abandoned music entirely.

The folk/blues boom of the early 1960s led to an upsurge of interest in his work. Although he was an alcoholic, in poor health, and had not so much as picked up a guitar in five years, House attempted a comeback and was delighted by the newfound respect accorded to him by the young, white audiences of the era. Despite his fragile condition, the ageing bluesmaster recorded a triumphant swansong, *Son House: The Legendary Father of Folk/Blues*, released by Columbia in 1965. He continued to perform until 1974, before retiring to Detroit – where he died in 1988.

Just as Son House had sought out early Charley Patton records, Jack White set about scouring the mustier corners of Detroit's record stores to advance his blues education. This was a task he took to with compulsive enthusiasm, but it was easy to soak up the local vibe.

Detroit's musical pedigree is as diverse as it is expansive. Since the 1960s, the city has provided the setting for the growth of Motown, the revolutionary rock of the MC5, the drug-fuelled hedonism of the Stooges, and the birth of techno. In addition to producing Bob Seger, Alice Cooper, George Clinton, Kid Rock and Eminem, Detroit has long been established as a centre of rough-hewn garage rock.

I know that's blasphemous when you are from Detroit, but I was never a fan of Motown stuff. I don't care for the production much. *Jack White*

The Hideout, a teen club that opened in 1964, became the epicentre of a local wave of sonic anarchy that soon spread as several new clubs opened up nearby. Established garage acts such as the Sonics, the Kingsmen and the Strangeloves shared the stage with future stars such as Ted Nugent (with the Amboy Dukes), Mitch Ryder (the Detroit Wheels) and Iggy Pop (the Iguanas).

Although the Detroit garage rock scene of the 1980s declined in parallel to the city's worsening economic status, the tradition was maintained by bands such as the Gories, 3-D Invisible, and the Hysteric Narcotics, all of whom developed enthusiastic local followings. A fan of the Sonics and the Stooges, Jack recognised the singular nature of his home town's rock scene: 'It's been like this for years, ever since I was old enough to go to shows. When I've gone to other towns, I've never seen rock 'n' roll bands like they have here. It's been amazing and I have no idea why.'

Matt Smith, a local record producer and guitarist with garage psychedelicists Outrageous Cherry, offered a geographical explanation: 'People here play as if the last 30 years of American culture never happened. You'll try out a guitar player and it's like he's never heard anything since 1972.'

Likewise, Jack indicated that a sense of separation lies at the core of the regional scene. 'Because it's an isolated place, it's got a lot of social outcasts going through their lives uninterested in mainstream culture. I'm not trying to sound romantic about the city but it's like you can do anything you want here, you can come up with an artistic idea and you can actually get it across to people, whereas in New York or Los Angeles you can't do that. There's too much going on, too many different areas in the city and there's 50,000 bands or artists or painters.'

In addition to a physical sense of dislocation, Detroit's rockers tended to operate in a political vacuum. Despite the collapse of the local motor manufacturing industries, and the social consequences of the resultant mass unemployment, few local groups have adopted a politicised stance – apart from the MC5, with their White Panther posturing.

Jack himself had little interest in politics. 'When I was a teenager, I was really into voicing my political opinions. But I could never see anything coming from it. The people who were organising the rallies and everything, I started to notice that they lived for dissatisfaction. And that is not me. The blues could be very political, you know – Lead Belly sang about Hitler. But I shy away from doing anything like that because I'm scared of novelty. I'm scared of having nowhere to go with it.'

As Jack's passion for delving deep into the musicology of the blues widened his influences, he expanded his technical capabilities by learning to play the piano. His parents had an old upright model that he began tinkering with. 'I taught myself how to play it,' he explained. 'I don't really know what it is I'm doing. I've got this thumb-and-pinkie technique and I just base things off of that. I know how I want it to sound.'

His growing interest in country

Iggy and the Stooges: 'The sound of Detroit eating its tail.'

music led him to the resophonic guitar, or 'dobro' – a horizontal steel-fretted guitar. The next eighteen months saw Jack learning his trade, developing his musical skills, and obsessively pursuing the roots of the blues. Christening themselves Two Part Resin, after the epoxy solvent used in upholstering, the Muldoon-Gillis duo continued with regular sessions, occasionally making four-track recordings of their output. It was from these tapes that a seven-inch single, credited to the Upholsterers and thematically titled 'Makers Of High Grade Suites', surfaced on the Sympathy for the Record Industry label some years later. 'The Upholsterers is just a one time art project,' explained Jack 'Both Brian Muldoon and I are upholsterers so we've talked about doing this record for a long time. We're both really proud of it.'

Jack was also developing an interest in art and design that would influence both his work and his wardrobe. As his knowledge of upholstery and furniture increased, he became fascinated by the aesthetic functionalism of the upholsterer's trade. Jack viewed skilled upholsterers as artists rather than tradesmen, and quickly acquired a distaste for the commercial aspects of the business. Instead, his regard for simplicity and directness drew him to the work of the Dutch 'De Stijl' (The Style) movement.

Founded in 1917 around the work and theory of architect Theo van Doesberg, De Stijl advocated the reduction of form to its simplest elements, limiting the palette to a fixed number of colours and eliminating all decorative aspects. The striking geometric paintings of Piet Mondrian and the furniture design of Gerrit Rietveld represent classic examples of the mode. This emphasis on simplicity struck an immediate chord with Jack. 'I started really loving all these furniture designers, and I got into Gerrit Rietveld – he did "Red and Blue Chair", which is a super-important piece. That got me into the De Stijl movement. I thought that was great, how they broke things down to their simplest components.'

It was weird, knowing him at nineteen, and seeing this person who had all these really clear-cut goals and this real commitment and passion for how he wanted things to go in his life, musically and otherwise. I remember him saying, 'I really want to be proud of everything I do.' *Dan Miller – Goober and the Peas*

In 1994, Jack returned to the drums to audition for the Detroit cow-punk band Goober and the Peas. Formed in the late 1980s, the band was led by singer/saxophonist Dan 'Goober' Miller, and had been compared to such bands as the Gun Club and Jason and the Scorchers. Incorporating a variety of styles, ranging from country-tinged swing to balls-out garage punk, Goober and the Peas had become regulars on the Detroit circuit and released two albums, *The Complete Works Of Goober And The Peas* and *The Jet Age Genius Of Goober And The Peas*, before splitting in 1995.

Despite being significantly younger than the rest of the quintet, Jack's earnest passion impressed Miller enough for him to take Jack on. Irrespective of his technical limitations as a drummer, Miller recalls Jack's early performances with some fondness: 'I do remember the first show when he played drums: For an encore he came up and sang some Elvis song. People where just shocked by his passion for it.'

The newly re-christened Jack 'Doc' Gillis became the latest in a long line of short-lived Goober and the Peas drummers. This was typical of the Detroit garage rock scene, where band personnel were often interchangeable and groups morphed into new incarnations almost at will. Although he found the live constraints of repeatedly playing the same set in the same way frustrating, Jack's tenure in the band provided him with valuable experience. 'I think it was a good thing for him just to see what it was like to be in a band that toured,' posited Miller, 'and probably see what kind of mistakes we made.' During this period Jack continued to work and jam with Brian Muldoon, who could see the benefits of Miller's influence on his young charge: 'He learned a lot about being on stage while playing in bands with Dan Miller – how to present himself, how to dress himself.'

Miller was one of several prominent figures around the Detroit scene who would play some part in Jack's continuing musical development. Perhaps the most established of these musicians was Mick Collins, the leader of the city's most influential underground band, the Gories. Often credited with being the 'Godfather' of modern Detroit garage rock, Miller formed the Gories as a trio in 1986, establishing the bass-less motif as a signature element of what would be sporadically referred to as the 'Detroit Sound'. The

The Detroit Godfather: Mick Collins of the Dirtbombs.

trio was rounded out by a second guitarist, Dan Kroha, and his girlfriend Peggy O'Neill on drums.

Jack's nephew, Ben Blackwell (who was to hook up with Collins as drummer in his later project, the excellent Dirtbombs), recalled, 'Jack really looks up to the Gories. He bought [the Hentchmen's third album] *Broad Appeal* and Mick Collins was behind him in line. And Jack was all excited – "Mick Collins was just behind me in line!"'

The Gories' unique primitivism was comprised of fuzzed-up garage punk in the mould of the Cramps, with an R&B edge influenced by Detroit vocalists such as Nolan Strong (of the Diablos) and Andre 'Mr. Rhythm' Williams (who had worked with Ike Turner at Motown, and with whom Collins would later collaborate on Williams' *Silky* album). The Gories produced a primal, echo-drenched form of junkyard garage that initially met a horrified reaction from gig-goers used to something more musical.

'People hated us, and we didn't care,' chuckled Collins. However, the band kept turning up for shows and gradually built up an enthusiastic local following. It included Jack White, who had been quick to pick up the Gories' debut album, *House Rockin'*, when it appeared on the Wanghead label in 1989. The band released two further albums, *I Know You Fine, But How You Doin'* and *Outta Here*, before Collins left to form the Blacktops in 1993.

One element of the Gories' mesmeric, lo-fi sleaze-rock that left an impression was the distinctive drum technique favoured by Peggy O'Neill. Like a reductive version of the Velvet Underground's Maureen Tucker, O'Neill hammered out a steady tom-tom beat, devoid of fills, with childlike innocence and simplicity. Through an accident of necessity, the Gories also had no bassist.

It underlined Jack's experiences of playing with Muldoon, listening to solo guitarists, and regarding the bass guitar as just an extraneous embellishment. 'Some songs don't need to have bass and some don't need all that drumming,' he later observed. 'In art, knowing where to stop is so important. I'm still learning. I'll see some bands that'll start out with drums, then they'll add bass. Then they should probably stop most times. But then they get another guitar and keyboard player, etc. Then you're like, 24, 36 tracks . . . It's scary. I mean, Mondrian's paintings. How simple they are compared to things these days? He just captured simplicity in them.'

Jack's projection of the De Stijl ethos onto a musical framework would cause him to become wary of too much elaboration. 'There's a lot of garage rock bands in Detroit, and if they write a riff they mess it up by covering it up with so much complication. Whereas I thought they should just play the same riff over and over *without* three guitars and a drummer trying to cover each other up. If there was just one guitar and that pounding drum, then there'd be *no way* you could ignore that riff.'

'Doc' Gillis' tenure as Goober and the Peas' drummer came to an end a few months before the group split for good in 1995. Growing increasingly dissatisfied with his role in the band, Jack opted to strike out on his own. 'I felt like I wasn't expressing myself enough, and that I was just being walked all over. People were telling me what to do all the time. Drummers always get the short end of the stick. No matter how great you are, or how simple you are, you get shafted.'

For Dan Miller, Jack's departure came as no great surprise. 'I know one of the things that was frustrating for him back with Goober and the Peas is he'd want to change songs night to night, even as the drummer. But that's hard when you have five people in the band.'

Unfazed by the disappointment of losing another sticksman, Miller paid testament to Jack's commitment, 'He was always passionate about keeping things fresh, keeping the inspiration. If we practiced a song a few times in a row, it would be played three different ways. And maybe one way would be horrible, but at least he took the risk of trying something that came into his head.'

Although his first experience of playing with a touring band ended in frustration, Jack's time with Goober and the Peas benefitted his musical education. He now had first-hand experience of life on the road, had picked up tips on stagecraft, and was developing ideas about the direction he wished to follow. Being in the band also provided an entrée to the Detroit scene – where, in addition to rubbing shoulders with musicians he admired, he also met a number of people who were to play a significant part in his future. One of whom was a shy catering student and part-time waitress named Meg White.

Why get a bass player? Why add more stuff when it is already truthful. *Jack White*

Megan Martha White was born in Detroit on 10 December 1974. Her parents, Walter Hackett White Jr., and his wife Catherine Della, lived in the prosperous suburb of Grosse Point, situated on the coast to the east of the city. Small and shy, Meg passed through school without making any kind of impression.

'It was a pretty normal childhood. I was very, very shy,' she recalled. 'Back then, I was shy to the point where I didn't speak. I guess I'm just not so good at socialising. Other than that, it was pretty normal.'

Like Jack, Meg was a solitary child, who enjoyed nothing more than to reconstruct Superman's Fortress of Solitude in the back yard. 'I would shovel up all the winter snow into a big mountain and then tunnel all the way through. I was obsessed with it. It was the best.'

Despite a brief flirtation with the violin, she showed no great musical inclination and kept her own company, 'I've always kind of lived in my own world,' she later admitted, 'everything else outside me seems far, far away.'

After leaving high school, Meg enrolled in catering college and took on some part-time work in order to make ends meet. One such job was a bartending stint at the Royal Oak, a blues 'n' barbecue joint that was part of the Detroit underground circuit. Although by no means as obsessive as Jack, Meg took an interest in music and attended local gigs. It was at a Goober and the Peas show that she and Jack are believed to have first met.

Given their similarly quiet and unassuming natures, and shared interest in vintage music, it was natural that the pair would hit it off. They quickly began spending increasing amounts of time together and a relationship soon blossomed. Detroit concert promoter Greg Baise recalls encountering the couple: 'I worked at Car City Records, at 8-mile and Harper, in the mid-1990s. Meg lived in the neighbourhood and would come in and buy records all the time. One day she showed up with her boyfriend – or fiancé. Back then he had blond hair, really curly. They'd come in and do what everybody does at Car City – go through the vinyl bins looking for good records, both popular records and more obscure things as well.'

Meanwhile, in addition to quitting Goober and the Peas, Jack had moved on from Muldoon Upholstery to the larger Beaupre Studios. Although he was no longer working with Brian Muldoon, the two of them remained friends and continued to regularly jam together.

> ### Three can be translated in so many ways. There's the trinity in Christianity, and objects in the world: a traffic light. A table can have only three legs and stand up. Or a wheel on a car can have only three nuts to hold it on. There's a definition about that. *Jack White*

Jack's parents had also decided to sell their house on Ferdinand Avenue, so Jack agreed to buy it – taking on additional freelance work in order to help with the upkeep. It quickly proved to be a less than satisfactory arrangement. Irritated by the limitations of commercial upholstery, Jack decided to open his own studio. He rented some space and, drawing on the principles of De Stijl, adopted a fixed three-colour scheme as his personal motif.

Having painted the entire workshop yellow, white and black, Jack kitted himself out in a natty set of yellow and black overalls. A loan of $1200 paid for a Ford van from a local used-car dealership. It was yellow. Finally, with his obsessive eye for detail, Jack set about ensuring that all his power and hand tools complied with the yellow/white/black motif.

Although eye-catching, Jack's artistic ideas often baffled his clients. 'I got so much into the cartooniness of the business,' he admitted, 'almost to the point of it being a joke to the people who would see me, and they wouldn't really trust me to do a good job.'

The rationale behind Jack's choice of three colours is explained by his long held, perhaps compulsive fascination with the number itself. As with his discovery of the blues, Jack's numerological fascination has its origins in a moment of revelation. 'There was a piece of fabric over part of a couch. The guy I was working for put in three staples. You couldn't have one or two, but three was the minimum way to upholster something. And

Meg and Jack play at the Radio 1 'One Big Weekend' event at Heaton Park, Manchester.

it seemed things kept revolving around that. Like, you only need to have three legs on a table . . . the three components of songwriting [storytelling, melody and rhythm], the three chords of rock 'n' roll or the blues . . .'

Similarly, the significance attached by blues mythology to the 'seventh son' keyed directly into Jack's numerological leanings – often claiming to be a seventh son himself. It has its origin in ancient civilisations: the Egyptians, for example, worshipped seven gods, whereas Buddhists appropriated the concept of seven stages of spiritual development from the Aryans of India.

This numerology was assimilated into a wide spectrum of supernatural belief systems such as Christianity (whose followers believe the world was created in seven days) and the Tarot (where the number is perceived as having spiritual and contemplative properties). The idea that a seventh son of a seventh son is in some way special is also referred to in the Christian Bible, and it's from this source that the concept found its way into the pan-cultural melting pot of blues mythology. This is exemplified by Willie Mabon's 1955 hit 'Seventh Son'.

Why can't people just write about the music? Why do people have to worry about our personal lives? *Jack White*

The number three also has a long and diverse history of being imbued with importance by different cultures. Maintaining this high concept, the new business was named 'Third Man Upholstery', with yellow, black and white business cards printed which bore the company slogan: 'Your Furniture's Not Dead.'

With additional embellishment provided by a furniture tack and a spatter of blood-red paint, the cards tended to put customers off. Jack was disappointed by their bemusement, but understood the reaction. 'I started trying to make an art form out of giving someone a bill for my services, like writing it with crayon on a piece of paper, or having a yellow piece of paper with black marker saying, "You owe me $300." . . . . People just didn't dig it. It was two different worlds colliding. When I'd re-upholster furniture I'd take off the old fabric and I started to write poems and things inside the furniture, so if it was ever re-upholstered again one day they'd get little messages from the last person who upholstered it.'

When not engaged in his own private upholsterer's revolution, or jamming with Brian Muldoon, Jack found time to see plenty of Meg. They'd become increasingly close, and, with both of them being romantically and traditionally inclined, decided to get married. Witnessed by Muldoon and Meg's sister, Heather, the couple were wed in South Lyon, Michigan on 9 September 1996. Unconventionally, Jack opted to take Meg's surname.

Neither party has ever publicly explained the reason for this (although 'the Gillis

Stripes' doesn't work as well). Similarly, the duo have always maintained a firm-but-dignified refusal to discuss aspects of their relationship, their families or their private lives. Any interviewer who attempts a line of probing personal enquiry is likely to encounter a resolute silence.

Jack found it difficult to understand why anyone would be interested in the duo as personalities rather than musicians, 'We've done a lot of interviews lately, and so many of them have absolutely nothing to do with music,' he told *Filter* magazine. 'They just keep asking all these sort of celebrity questions . . . . And then people get mad at us like, "Oh you guys don't like to answer those questions." My response is, "Do you?" Someone's interviewing you about your job and they end up asking you what clothes you wear to work in the morning. It doesn't mean anything.'

Similarly, Meg saw little value in fandom, outside of an aesthetic appreciation of the work itself. 'I don't want to know about my biggest idols. I don't want to read their autobiographies, I don't want to find out what they're really like.'

A moderate traditionalist at heart, Jack's distaste for the media celebrity circus is at best lightly veiled. While it may be frustrating for fans used to a culture of invasive reportage and mock-horror tabloid moralising, the White Stripes' refusal to discuss their intimate details has had mixed results. Although the embargo has served to focus journalistic emphasis on their music, it has also heightened unfounded speculation, especially about Jack and Meg's relationship.

'The one thing the fucking media hates is not being able to dissect someone,' Jack would later assert, 'so that every little part of their existence can be written as a sound bite in a paragraph . . . that's not what you need to know about, that's got nothing to do with the music we make. What we create, you can talk about. What the songs are, how we present them live, and what the aesthetic is, art-wise, to what we're creating.'

Following his nuptials, Jack maintained his relationship with Dan Miller by hooking up with the vocalist's post-Goober band, 2 Star Tabernacle. The group also included Miller's wife Tracee on bass, and future Detroit Cobras drummer Damian Lang. Combining elements of country, blues and rock, 2 Star Tabernacle touched base with most of Jack's influences, and the quartet commenced regular rehearsals. By the end of 1996 the new group were ready to perform in public.

minimum r&b

2

It's hard for me, because I'm constantly battling what's good and bad about ego. *Jack White*

With the newlyweds settled into Ferdinand Avenue, Jack divided his time between rehearsing with 2 Star Tabernacle and running Third Man Upholstery. Deprived of his former apprentice, Brian Muldoon also found himself increasingly busy.

The Upholsterers sessions dried up completely. What little spare time remained to Jack was divided between catching the occasional local gig, absorbing old country, blues and folk records, and writing new material in his attic. Without Muldoon, Jack's home sessions lacked a rhythm element to underscore his explosive fuzz-blues salvos. Finding this frustrating, the guitarist asked his new wife to sit at the drum kit and beat out time. In revelatory fashion, the seed that would become the White Stripes was sown.

'Our sound came the first time we tried it,' Jack revealed. 'I played a riff, and Meg joined in on the toms. It felt good to try to do something simple but make it as powerful as possible.' The addition of Meg's untutored drumming to Jack's virtuoso pyrotechnics keyed directly into the guitarist's notions of simplicity and completed his 'trinity' of storytelling, rhythm and melody.

As well as being a creative landmark, the duo's first session also produced 'Screwdriver' – a song that was to appear on their debut album, and still regularly turns up in their live shows. 'We were just goofing around,' recalled Jack. 'We just started doing this riff and there was this screwdriver laying there in the room so I started singing about it – what I'd do with it – you know, being angry. We thought it sounded really good and we thought, "Why don't we work on this?"'

Irrespective of her passing acquaintance with the violin and love of music, Meg had no previous experience of the drums. Nor had she ever considered becoming a drummer. She later joked that any enthusiasm for her instrument 'came after when Jack tied me to the drum set'. Shy and reserved, Meg required a degree of persuasion before she agreed to expand the marital partnership to include band rehearsals.

Any protestations about lack of technique were instantly dismissed by Jack, who was captivated with the childlike directness of her simple beats. 'It was kind of nice that she didn't know what she was doing at first because our stuff was able to remain so simple. We still try to keep it that way. Meg never does drum fills or solos or anything like that. And I just love that drumming style. It's really cool to work off of, to play guitar off of, and to sing off.'

Jack's experiences with Muldoon and Goober and the Peas had taught him the disadvantages of larger ensembles, and even bigger ego clashes. 'Playing with another guy always leads into competitiveness,' he averred. 'Everyone I'd ever played with were, like,

The White Stripes in June 2002: 'as potent as rock gets,' said the **Guardian** *newspaper.*

male drummers who'd got the whole routine down, but Meg was playing so childishly, because she'd never even tried before.'

The closeness between Jack and Meg enabled an instinctive creative understanding. 'We have good communication between us, which helps us figure out what we want to do,' explained Jack. 'Because there's just the two of us in the band it means the music is less structured and can be more "on the moment"'.

All of Jack White's major influences were firmly rooted in the notion of simplicity. Whether it was the basic combination of vocals and guitar that comprised much of blues, country and folk, or the aesthetic restraint of De Stijl, the guitarist found himself drawn toward reductive forms of expression.

We can be very honest, and even if we scream and yell at each other we'll still love each other. *Jack White*

Similarly, Jack viewed childhood as a blessed state of innocence and simplicity: 'I like looking at things from a child's point of view, trying to get as honest as possible. Children who are really young don't lie. When they get older, they start being untruthful, start dressing how everyone else dresses, start worrying about what everyone else thinks. I like those periods of life before it gets to the point where other people are corrupting your viewpoint.'

Meg's minimalist drumming and naive demeanour added her own childlike aspect. Remove Meg from the equation and the element that makes the White Stripes unique is likewise removed. Accomplished solo guitarists will always be around, whereas male/female guitar and drum duos (of widely differing technical abilities) are an absolute novelty. 'I love Meg's innocence and her childishness,' declared Jack. 'And whether that's a feminine characteristic that's disregarded or degraded or whatever . . . Or maybe it's not even a feminine characteristic at all. Maybe I could be that way just as easily. But I love that, and I think that's the most important part of the band. Almost everything we do is based around her. It wouldn't be the White Stripes without her. If it was some guy in the band, it wouldn't work.'

Always quick to convert abstract ideas into physical actions, Jack set about incorporating the theme of childhood innocence into the framework of the group. As he later explained, 'the band started off as a real childish idea, as a real childish band. Like little kids playing instruments.'

The association between children and candy presented the duo with both their visual image and their name. 'Meg loves peppermints, and we were going to call ourselves the Peppermints,' Jack recalled. 'But since our last name was White, we decided to call it the White Stripes. It revolved around this childish idea; the ideas kids have – because they are so much better than adult ideas, right? And we thought it would be a good stage aesthetic to dress in the colours of the peppermint, so that people would think like kids when they saw us, or at least remember who we were.'

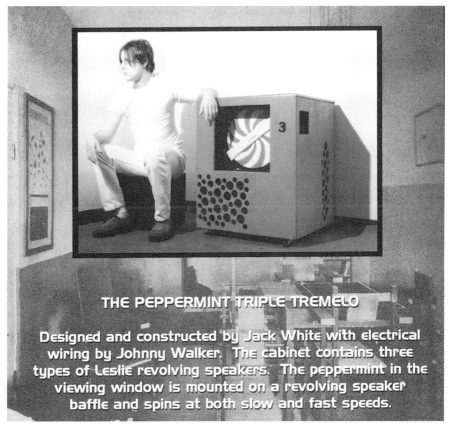

THE PEPPERMINT TRIPLE TREMELO

Designed and constructed by Jack White with electrical
wiring by Johnny Walker. The cabinet contains three
types of Leslie revolving speakers. The peppermint in the
viewing window is mounted on a revolving speaker
baffle and spins at both slow and fast speeds.

Jack with his 'Peppermint Triple tremolo'.

In keeping with his obsession with the number three, Jack added black to the red and white candy cane motif. The duo began dressing exclusively in these colours, and the house at Ferdinand Avenue was redecorated to match. Jack's 1960s vintage Airline guitar was made to comply with the colour scheme, and Meg's bass drum was decorated with a peppermint swirl. Later, Jack would equip his speaker cabinet with a dual-speed revolving baffle inspired by the same candy cane design. Christened the 'Peppermint Triple Tremolo', the customised Leslie amplifier was re-built following a junkyard sortie. 'I found three different components in the garbage,' recalled Jack. 'I was trash picking and I built 'em all together and made a speaker cabinet out of it. It was just a nice project to work on.'

Although the White Stripes were developing a distinctive visual image, Ben Blackwell had doubts about the band's chosen name: 'When I first heard about them naming the band the White Stripes, I thought people were going to think they were a skinhead band. Originally they were tossing back and forth the names Bazooka and Soda Powder, so after hearing the other names they had come up with, the White Stripes didn't seem so bad.'

As the elements that would make up the White Stripes began to coalesce, Jack continued working with 2 Star Tabernacle. The guitarist had contributed future White Stripes numbers such as 'Now Mary', 'The Union Forever' and 'The Big Three Killed My Baby' to the quartet's repertoire. During the first six months of 1997, the group played a number of small gigs around Detroit. Discouragingly, the local alternative music scene offered few venues where aspiring acts could strut their stuff. Licensing laws prohibited alcohol consumption to those under 21, displacing the younger audiences to coffee houses such as Zoot's and Planet Ant.

However, in 1996, the Gold Dollar (a former drag bar on Detroit's seedy Cass Corridor) was re-opened as a live music venue, and provided local bands such as the Detroit Cobras, Rocket 455 and the Hentchmen with a showcase more suited to their untrammelled garage rock. After acquiring the dilapidated building from its previous owner, new landlord Neil Yee set about renovating the space with the assistance of friends, dates and whoever happened to be hanging around. A drummer with experience in sound engineering, Yee favoured a creative booking policy that gave exposure to some eclectic and diverse performers. The grand opening took place on 8 August 1996, featuring music from Twitch and the performance of an original 'playlet', *The Red Geranium*. The small bar (legal capacity 107) was largely staffed by Yee's friends, who included Meg's sister, Heather.

In addition to offering a mixture of films, performance and rock, the Gold Dollar had a regular open-mike night that took place every Thursday. It was at one of these shows, on 14 July 1997, that the White Stripes made their live debut.

Whereas Jack could draw on his concert experiences with Goober and the Peas, and latterly with 2 Star Tabernacle, Meg was an absolute novice. As she later told the *Detroit Free Press*, 'We did our first show two months after I started playing.' The thinking behind performing at an all-comers' show was that it would allow her to get used to being on stage, in preparation for a gig Jack had arranged with Yee for the following month.

You know how whenever you do something you think, 'Oh yeah, I'm having fun and I'm doing something I love. But no one's going to like this.' But then when people really like it, then what do you do? *Jack White*

'There was only, like, ten or fifteen people there,' recalled Jack. 'We played three songs, one of which was "Love Potion Number Nine". We were shocked that people dug what we were doing.'

Ben Blackwell was on hand to tape the show, and was suitably impressed: 'I had made a copy of their first show at the Gold Dollar and listened to that tape forever. I remember singing "Screwdriver" and "Jimmy The Exploder" over and over. By the time the first record did finally come out, I was tired of the songs because I'd been listening to those songs for two years.'

On 14 August, the duo were booked as support to local favourites Rocket 455. With his hair dyed red for the occasion, Jack set about constructing a visual image for the band by arranging various red and white items (including a backdrop) around the stage. The show was moderately attended. As Neil Yee would later explain, 'If the number of people who were there who have since claimed they were at that gig [were actually there], they would have played the Pontiac Silver Dome.'

The following night, at the Gold Dollar, the White Stripes supported bass-less garage rockers the Hentchmen and local sixties revivalists Insect. Willy Wilson, a local DJ with WDET-FM, declared himself immediately impressed with Jack and Meg's performance: 'It was fun at their first shows, being one of twenty or so people there. It was really sloppy and stripped down, because Meg really couldn't play. But it was fun and interesting. There was something unique there, because you could tell that the songs Jack was doing stood out. It was better songwriting.'

The whole point is to sell out without looking like you're selling out. Everyone has a price. If they haven't signed yet, it's because they haven't got their price yet. *Neil Yee*

Delighted with the immediate response accorded the band, a happy Jack enthused, 'When me and Meg started playing in Detroit, we didn't have any friends. And we thought people were going to hate us. We started going to shows and met people into sort of garage rock. And they seemed like real obscurists, real record-collector-type people. When we first played we thought, "Aw, we're not doing any particular thing." But people immediately loved us. The first show – I couldn't believe it. And all of a sudden we had friends and people to talk to.'

With his latest venture now a viable live concern, Jack divided his creative energies between the White Stripes, 2 Star Tabernacle and guest appearances as bassist with the Hentchmen. The low maintenance required to get a two-piece band on stage meant it was often possible for Jack and Meg to appear as support act for Jack's other projects.

However, as Ben Blackwell explained, promoters often struggled with the duo's name: 'I drove down with them to see a show at Frankie's in Toledo where there was no more than ten people watching. They were opening for 2 Star Tabernacle and were mis-billed that night as the "White Lines". Of course, that wasn't as bad as when they played the Magic Bag one night and were billed as the "Light Strikes".'

There was no such confusion at the Gold Dollar, which by the end of 1997 had become a home venue to all of Jack's bands. The bar was developing a reputation as the fulcrum of Detroit's independent music scene, and local record label proprietors such as Dave Buick (Italy Records) and Andy and Patti Claydon (Flying Bomb) were regular attendees. Buick, who was a bassist with Detroit sleaze-rockers The Go and later played in the Lost Kids with Ben Blackwell, had recently founded the label with a view to promoting local talent.

Recalling his introduction to the band, Buick explained, 'I was at the first two White

Big sister keeps the beat – Meg maintains her concentration at the Gold Dollar.

Stripes shows and the majority of the fans were outside the Gold Dollar while they were playing . . . I'd told all these people, "You gotta come see the White Stripes," and they were like, "Nah, the singer annoys me. He whines – it's annoying." And then a couple of months later, they were saying, "Man, I've been listening to it, and this stuff is really, really good."'

Italy Records' first release was a Rocket 455 single, 'Ain't That Right Girl', and Buick was keen to add the White Stripes to his roster. 'At the end of '97 I confronted [Jack] about putting out a single. And he was immediately like, "Nah, no, no, I can't afford it," and walked away. He didn't understand at first that I was offering to pay for it.'

'Let's Shake Hands' – the White Stripes' debut single for Italy Records.

Undaunted by Jack's initial refusal, Dave Buick made a second attempt at enticing the White Stripes onto Italy Records. Once it was made clear to Jack that the cost of recording and pressing the single would be borne by the label, his unwillingness evaporated. For convenience, as well as to keep the production costs down, sessions for the single were recorded at Ferdinand Avenue. Released in April 1998, 'Let's Shake Hands' is a thunderous slice of discordant garage blues. Jack's anxious vocals struggle to escape the gravitational well created by his string bending, while Meg's percussive supernovas explode across a fuzztone soundscape. The track was backed with 'Look Me Over Closely' – a Marlene Dietrich number from 1953. 'I had just bought the LP on a lark and loved that song. A cool 1930s Broadway type thing,' explained Jack.

The record was recorded by Jeff Meier and produced by Buick under the pseudonym of 'David Italy'. 1000 copies of the single were pressed on appropriately red vinyl and distributed via local record stores, at gigs and by Buick via mail order. The sleeve featured a Heather White picture of the couple, which showed an extraordinarily young-looking Jack sporting his red hair-do.

In July, after their first headline appearance at the Gold Dollar (supported by the Soledad Brothers – a gutbucket blues outfit named after a political alliance formed by black convicts in prison), the White Stripes accepted an invitation from Andy Claydon to record a track for the second volume of his Flying Bomb label's *Surprise Package* Christmas sampler. Established by the Claydons in 1996, Flying Bomb had released singles by most of the Detroit garage heavyweights.

In addition to the Hentchmen, the Gories-inspired Bantam Rooster, and Mick Collins' Dirtbombs, the label was home to The Wildbunch – who would later morph into the Electric Six to have massive hits with 'Danger (High Voltage)' and 'Gay Bar'.

A prototype version of 'Danger (High Voltage)' can be found on the Wildbunch's first single, 'The Ballad of MC Sucka DJ'. The band had also been included (alongside the Dirtys and Bantam Rooster) on Flying Bomb's first Yuletide *Surprise Package*.

For the 1998 edition, the White Stripes recorded 'Candy Cane Children', a track that would be re-released by XL Records in 2002 as the A-side of the limited edition single 'Merry Christmas From The White Stripes'. More brooding than 'Let's Shake Hands', 'Candy Cane Children' revealed Jack's blues-inspired lyrical fascination with the broken-hearted lover, albeit in a suitably festive context.

I put out the first two singles. Jack always had long-term plans for the White Stripes . . . That whole first year, every single person misprinted the band name – it was always 'White Stripe' or 'White Strike' or 'White Strikes'. It never got printed right, for a whole year. *Dave Buick*

The sampler was released as a three-track seven-inch EP, which featured Rocket 455's 'Santa Ain't Coming For Christmas' as the A-side, with 'Candy Cane Children' and the Blowtops 'Sidewalk Santa' on the reverse. The track was mixed by Jim Diamond at Ghetto Records. Diamond (who would go on to play bass in Mick Collins' Dirtbombs) had relocated to Detroit in 1996 and established his studio in a disused poultry processing plant behind the State Theatre.

Although the studio lived up to its name – 'smelling of stale pizza, cold beer and carpet mould' – Diamond's relaxed and intuitive approach to production quickly established Ghetto as the Abbey Road of the Detroit garage underground. A 2 Star Tabernacle performance had set the scene for his first encounter with Jack, and although the producer later confessed that he 'never really liked that band', it marked the beginning of a collaborative relationship that endured throughout the first two White Stripes albums.

Six months after 'Let's Shake Hands', the duo released a second seven-inch single on Italy, 'Lafayette Blues'. Recorded at home by Jack (Ferdinand Avenue having been re-named 'Third Man Studios, South West Detroit') and mixed by Diamond, the single was another crashing collision between rock and blues, with a lyric based around Detroit's French street names.

The B-side, 'Sugar Never Tasted So Good', followed the pattern set by the previous release by showcasing the subtler side of the White Stripes' rootsy sound. Accompanied by Meg's rudimentary percussion, Jack's acoustic strumming and uncomplicated vocal reflected his country/folk influences. It also exemplified the childlike simplicity that had become the duo's signature. Once again, the track would later resurface on the White Stripes' debut album.

1000 copies of 'Lafayette Blues' were pressed on what was supposed to be white vinyl. However, at the pressing plant, the residue of a previous coloured pressing remained in the machinery and mixed with the vinyl prepared for the single. Serendipitously, the rogue colour happened to be red. It gave the pressing some unique qualities, as the red/white mix was inconsistent: the discs pressed earlier in the run contained more red than those produced later on. A further accidental enhancement occurred due to the late arrival of the sleeves with their candy-coloured design. Keen to sell the record at a Gold Dollar show supporting the Hentchmen, Jack and Dave Buick hand-painted covers for fifteen copies of the record. These sold for $6 on the night, but are now showing up on internet auction sites for well over $500.

Away from the White Stripes, November 1998 saw the release (on Bloodshot Records) of 2 Star Tabernacle's debut single: a cover of Hank Williams' 'Ramblin' Man', recorded in collaboration with Andre Williams. Backed with one of Williams' 1960s compositions, 'Lily White Mama And Jet Black Daddy', it was recorded once again at Third Man Studios by Jeff Meier, and produced by former Gories guitarist Dan Kroha.

Jack, who had provided both piano and 'dobro' on the single, had wanted Williams to record some original material with the band and had offered him 'The Big Three Killed My Baby' – one of the White Stripes' most effective early numbers. At the time, he perceived his work for both bands to be of equal status. Williams, perhaps mindful of the potential for royalties, preferred to record his own material. The track would later emerge as the first single to be taken from *The White Stripes*.

If anyone asks you people who sang you this song, just tell them it's Jackie White, he's done been here and gone, he's just looking for a home. *Jack White, from 'Boll Weevil'*

Reviewing 'Ramblin' Man' for *The Michigan Daily*, arts correspondent Gabe Fajuri was disappointed by 2 Star Tabernacle's apparent reluctance to record any of their own songs: 'Overall, the record provides lightning quick and frankly disappointing introduction to one of Detroit's more interesting bands. The work is not the Tabernacle's own, and not a good representation of its work. Hopefully, 2 Star Tabernacle will release a full-length record of original material in the near future. Hardcore fans of the local indie-country (or "insurgent country") movement will have to wait until then to find something worthwhile from their hometown heroes.'

During the same period, Jack's occasional bass duties with the Hentchmen saw him featured on their *Hentch-Forth* nine-track mini-album and 'Some Other Guy' single, which were also released by Italy Records.

The release of 'Let's Shake Hands' and 'Lafayette Blues', along with a string of memorable shows, had established the White Stripes as a presence on the Detroit scene. Among the pre-eminent bands on the local circuit (along with the Hentchmen and the Detroit Cobras) were The Go, an MC5-inspired ensemble fronted by vocalist 'Howlin'' Bobby Harlow that also featured Dave Buick on bass.

Accompanied by guitarist John Krautner, Harlow decided to take in a 2 Star Tabernacle show. As he later recalled, the singer was immediately struck by Jack's performance – 'Jack was laying back playing great guitar, singing harmonies with Dan Miller. He just had a great stage presence – he looked really cool, he looked comfortable. He wasn't a phoney at all. I said to John, "Let's go up front and look at this guy." Dave Buick had already put out a White Stripes single at that point. Dave and Jack were buddies. Later, Jack was over at Dave's house, so John and I went over there: "Hey, Jack, we've got a question for you – " And Jack said, "Yes, already, yes, absolutely, wanna join, count me in." We said, "All right!"'

With Jack's creativity now finding a third outlet, rehearsals with The Go went well. The band were attracting interest from Sub Pop, the Seattle label who first signed Nirvana, and work on a prospective debut album was already well underway.

The rehearsals that took place at Ferdinand Avenue left a lasting impression on Bobby Harlow: 'Whenever we practiced at Jack's house, we practiced upstairs in his room. For the record: Jack's house is red and white. The whole damned thing is red and white. The attic – the practice room – has got an American flag, all done in red and white. He's full-blown.'

For his part, Jack was delighted to have joined the group. 'They'd been looking for a lead guitar player, I thought this was the band that I always wanted to be in.' As much of the material that would ultimately be included on The Go's debut album had already been written, Jack's contribution was largely limited to recording lead guitar sections once the band entered the studio with Jim Diamond and producer Matthew Smith. Nevertheless, two White compositions – 'Keep On Trash' and 'Time For The Moon' – can also be found on the LP.

During the early months of 1999, The Go remained Jack's creative focal point. The quartet played regular gigs before enthusiastic local audiences and a strong set of material was ready for inclusion on the album. However, the arrival of a contract offer placed Jack in an awkward situation. 'We were signing with Sub Pop – an exclusive contract,' Bobby Harlow explained. 'So it was a matter of whether Jack was going to be on the contract or not. Basically, if Jack had signed, that would have meant Sub Pop would have rights to the White Stripes stuff as well. Seemed like a bad idea. Jack had established the White Stripes as something he wanted to do. He was sort of teetering – "Should I sign, should I not?"'

It drove an immediate wedge between Jack, who was reluctant to cede control of the White Stripes to Sub Pop, and the rest of The Go – who were understandably keen to sign the deal and get things moving. Ultimately, Jack's association with The Go had to come to an abrupt end. His attitude was phlegmatic. 'I think it was part of God's plan.

There was no way it would have worked out. We would've disagreed all the time. We have different ways of looking at stuff.'

Although disappointed at losing such an incandescent lead guitarist, Dave Buick conceded the inevitability of the situation. 'So things ended. He was really good in The Go, but it probably worked out better – not for The Go, but for Jack.'

The Go's debut album, *Whatcha Doin'*, was released by Sub Pop in the summer of 1999 and included Jack's guitar contributions. A critical success, the record also found favour with the band's departed member. 'Those guys are amazing! And some of the songs on that album are really, really, really good,' he enthused. 'It was the best time I ever had. I wish I could've stayed.'

Unable to grasp rock 'n' roll aesthetics outside of their familiar grunge territory, Sub Pop's enthusiasm for The Go waned in the aftermath of *Whatcha Doin'*. When the label attempted to influence the band's direction it led to a creative impasse, followed by a parting of the ways. 'We are impossible to work with if a label wants to "guide" us,' explained Harlow. 'We don't want to listen to anybody, ever . . . . We didn't belong there. It was a mistake, but they were able to introduce us to our audience.'

Several line up changes later, the group signed to the UK based Lizard King label, and in 2003 released a self-titled second album. Irrespective of the manner in which

The Go: (l-r) Jack White, Bobby Harlow, Mark Felis, John Krautner (bassist Dave Buick is out of shot).

The Go's eponymous debut album.

label politics derailed The Go, Bobby Harlow later paid fulsome tribute to his more successful accomplice: 'Jack's my friend. He's a true grit individual. I'm sure, at times, that he misses dragging around with a bunch of wild-eyed misanthropes . . . but, such is life. I know he's doing well for himself and his "big sister" Meg. I was never that close with him during our time together in The Go, but now, occasionally we pass notes. He's the hardest working button to button.'

Jack's departure from The Go caused him to reconsider his direction. 'The White Stripes were getting pretty popular, and people were coming to see The Go and saying, "Oh, there's the guy from the White Stripes." It was taking away from the personality of the band. I wanted to do both. So I quit 2 Star Tabernacle, and The Go sort of kicked me out.' With his commitments greatly reduced, Jack focused all of his energies on the White Stripes.

Italy Records' limited reach restricted the impact of the White Stripes' first two singles to a local level. The initial pressings of each record would take around two years to sell out, and there was no question of the band making a national impact. Locally, it was a different story.

Reviewing 'Let's Shake Hands', the *Detroit Metro Times* offered encouragement: 'Get yourself acquainted with Jack and Meg White. "Let's Shake Hands", the A-side of this, the duo's first recorded foray, is a raucous invitation to do so. The crunched-out, Cramps-worthy riffage that the song is built upon is segmented by Jack White's plaintive, natural-as-breathing falsetto and the crashing waves of Meg White's cymbal, snare and bass drum punctuating the tender ruckus.'

We might get a roadie if we got that famous. That would be the one thing we'd change. *Jack White*

More significantly, a copy of the single had been passed to Sympathy for the Record Industry supremo Long Gone John, who had just released the Detroit Cobras' debut on his label. The White Stripes were offered an album deal, and, given that Italy Records' output was almost entirely confined to singles, unsurprisingly decided to accept.

Based in Long Beach, California, Sympathy for the Record Industry had established a reputation as both a fiercely independent and successful label. Founded in 1988, the label boasted a diverse back catalogue that included gloriously-monikered obscurities (Pigmy Love Circus, Vinyl Gang Bang), veteran rockers (Wreckless Eric, ex-Dead Boy Cheetah Crome, Mars Bonfire – writer of 'Born To Be Wild'), and latterly successful acts such as Hole, Bad Religion and Rocket From The Crypt.

Despite the label's prodigious output, it was essentially a one-man operation. A self-confessed 'Anti-mogul', Long Gone John selects bands in accordance with his personal tastes and oversees production and distribution. 'Lots of people think that Sympathy is a much bigger concern than it is,' he explained. 'People don't understand that it's just one person working out of his house, because I've always referred to "the staff at the Sympathetic Nerve Centre". People have called up and asked to speak to someone in the radio promotion department.'

Originally founded to enable garage punks the Lazy Cowgirls to release their live album, the label soon took on a life of its own. 'When I did that Lazy Cowgirls record, I had no intention of doing anything else,' recalled John. 'I was on my way out to Hollywood, I thought of the name for the label, and I thought that probably would be the only thing I would ever do. I had no design or interest in starting a record label. It was the same kind of situation for the next record. Then I started doing a bunch of seven-inches. Before I knew it, it was a real label.'

SFTRI quickly established maximum credibility as a purveyor of groundbreaking rock 'n' roll, and cemented its impeccable garage credentials by releasing a string of records by bands such as Thee Headcoats – an ensemble fronted by the maverick poly-math and underground garage genius, Billy Childish.

The signing of the White Stripes to Sympathy for the Record Industry made the band the latest in a series of Detroit acts to fall under Long Gone John's influence. In addition to the Cobras, White Stripes and Dirtbombs, John would subsequently issue material from other local bands such as Ko and the Knockouts, Bantam Rooster and the Von Bondies.

Despite this, he maintained that neither the city, nor his latest acquisitions, were in any way exceptional. 'Detroit isn't fucking special . . . the White Stripes weren't unique. I'd done 50, 60 bands like the White Stripes before the White Stripes. They're just another one that happened to hit and get some attention. They're not more talented, they're just lucky.'

Irrespective of John's faint praise, Jack was delighted to sign up. 'No one's telling us what to do, the artwork, what songs go on the album, he will do any seven-inches we want to do, anything.' Almost immediately, arrangements were made to record an album with Jim Diamond at Ghetto Records. Jack's rampant creativity and the duo's steady schedule of rehearsals and concerts ensured there was more than sufficient available material.

Recorded in under a week, using a basic sixteen-track set up at a cost of $2,000, the White Stripes' self-titled debut album was a testament to Jack's passion for simplicity. In order to capture the directness and authenticity that characterised many of his blues influences, Jack imposed a series of limitations on both the recording process and the band.

'I really felt like I had to find a way that I could play this music that felt so real and so cathartic for me . . . without getting this "white-boy blues" thing labelled on me,' explained the guitarist. 'Once [Meg and I] started playing rock and roll together, we sort of figured out this way of boxing ourselves in, so tight and so limited that you weren't really thinking about the notions behind it, it just felt more emotional.'

As well as using vintage equipment to produce a rootsy effect, Jack enforced strict rules limiting which particular instruments were used. 'Like I've made the rule in my life that I'm never going to learn how to play the harmonica. Even though I love the sound of the harmonica . . . . All of this – the band, the aesthetic, revolving around the num-

Even if the goal of achieving beauty from simplicity is aesthetically less exciting, it may force the mind to acknowledge the simple components that make the complicated beautiful. *Jack White*

ber three, the limitations – revolves around the most important thing about art to me, which is knowing when to stop. We set up this box where we created an idea of this band, the White Stripes, we sort of forced ourselves to live inside of it.'

Inherently influenced by De Stijl, and extended throughout every aspect of the band, Jack's reductionist vision was also a form of self-discipline. 'I like when people limit themselves. I love when artists do something with very little opportunity. I love forced creation. I used to own a record by William S. Burroughs, called *Break Through In Grey Room.* I always thought that was so great, just him in a room with a recording machine, cutting up the tape. I love that notion, anyone saying, "I'm going to set up rules for myself and live by them."'

In keeping with the emphasis on guitar, vocals and drums, the only additional instrumentation on *The White Stripes* (aside from Jack's keyboards on the duo's cover of Bob Dylan's 'One More Cup Of Coffee' and 'St James Infirmary Blues') was some back-up slide guitar provided by the Soledad Brothers' Johnny Walker on 'Suzy Lee' and 'I Fought Piranhas'. As the White Stripes' live show only required a basic drum kit, guitar and amp, additional equipment was borrowed from Dan Miller and Brian Muldoon. Of the seventeen songs recorded, fourteen were original compositions – with the duo's selection of cover versions reflecting their influences (Robert Johnson's 'Stop Breaking Down', Dylan's 'One More Cup Of Coffee' and 'St James Infirmary Blues', originally recorded by 1930s band leader Cab Calloway).

None of the songs released by Italy Records were recycled for the album, which provided further evidence of Jack's creative fecundity and the strength of the material he worked on with Muldoon and Miller. Aside from the tracks that surfaced at 2 Star Tabernacle and Upholsterers sessions, many of the songs had been written some time earlier – 'Sugar Never Tasted So Good' was composed as long ago as 1994.

Stylistically, the album established the parameters of the band's unique sound. Jack's ferocious guitar assault and hysterical vocal style is grounded by Meg's booming primitivism. Songs that would otherwise be simple combinations of rhythm and melody are imbued with savage intent by the raw emotion the duo bring to their music. Lyrically, Jack's preoccupation with childhood, discipline and integrity is well represented, the notion of the childlike given corporeal form by the uncluttered delivery.

'There's definitely a childishness in it,' asserted Jack. 'From Meg's standpoint, the drumming is real primitive and I really love that. My voice, I think, sometimes sounds like a little kid. You see that approach in a lot of great bands – Iggy Pop throwing tantrums on stage. Everybody's still that same person they were when they were young – at least they still want to be. They still want to have that freedom.'

The White Stripes was scheduled for release in June 1999, allowing ample time for post-production, design and promotion. As a teaser for the album, 'The Big Three Killed My Baby' was to be released as a single. The song was among Jack's favourites and, following Andre Williams' reluctance to record it at the 2 Star Tabernacle sessions, remained unreleased despite being a firm live favourite.

As well as epitomising Jack's fixation with the number three (the song has three verses, utilises three chords and is accented on the third beat), the lyrics express the writer's dislike of the automotive industry and its effects upon society. 'I hate cars,' Jack explained', 'and anything to do with them. That's the truth. The Big Three [Ford,

I was talking to some friends from New York the other day, and they were saying Detroit is a ghost town. But as Iggy Pop said – in Detroit you're one in a hundred; in New York or L.A., you're one in a million. *Jack White*

General Motors and Chrysler] have continuously ripped off the world for a hundred years, and it doesn't seem like it's gonna stop anytime soon.'

As a native of Detroit, Jack could hardly have failed to notice the impact of the decline of the industry on his home town. Faced with cheap overseas competition, Detroit's major motor manufacturers opted for mass redundancies in order to maximise profits. It sent the local economy into a downward spiral from which it has yet to recover.

'The city still looks as it did 30 years ago,' asserted Meg. 'Basically, there is no downtown. There's nobody on the streets. Downtown Detroit has more vacant buildings over ten storeys than any city in the world. Tons of skyscrapers with nothing in them.'

'A lot of people in the richer suburbs will say, "I've never been below 10 Mile Road,"' added Jack. '8 Mile's the border between downtown and the suburbs . . . I used to work various jobs and people'd go, "Where do you live?" "Oh, I live in south-west Detroit, the Mexican neighbourhood," and they'd be like, "You live down there?! Are you insane?!" I'm like, "Well, I've lived there my whole life." The animosity between the city and the suburbs is huge. It's like two different worlds.'

A series of howling gales whipped up by blues-driven frustration, 'The Big Three Killed My Baby' identifies the motor industry as the chief maggot in Detroit's decaying core. The song juxtaposes the iconic status of the automobile in American society with the human misery that is it's by-product.

'Everybody, all they do is spend all their money on the car companies,' declared Jack. 'It seems to be this thing that everybody just accepts, like that's the way it's gonna be, and nobody complains about it. I don't understand it.'

More personally, his own experiences as a motorist had reinforced his perspective. 'I think they are the worst money pits and killing machines of all time. Every car I've ever had has broken down, like, every week.' Warming to his theme, the guitarist pointed to two vaguely industrial looking rings and a bracelet. 'These are hose clamps from a car engine. I wear them as a symbol. I wanted to organise an anti-automotive festival in Detroit, but it never came together. It's such a farce. The companies are so tied in with the oil companies. For God's sake, we have wars over the oil to put gas in our cars.'

An additional track, 'Red Bowling Ball Ruth', was selected for the B-side of the new single. The song was not included on the album and had not originally been earmarked for release. Initially, their cover of Robert Johnson's 'Stop Breaking Down' had been intended to back up 'The Big Three Killed My Baby', to make it, as Jack said, 'a whole anti-automotive 45'.

'Then when we recorded it, it came out so good we figured we'd better put it on the album.' Despite being influenced by the Rolling Stones, Jack was unaware of their version of the song. 'I'd heard *Exile on Main Street* before but didn't own it and so had actually never heard the Rolling Stones version of "Stop" until after our LP came out.'

Viewed as an overall work, *The White Stripes* is modern music laid bare. The duo's rock, blues, country and folk influences are distilled into a series of unembellished songs that precisely capture the emotional intent. Opening with twenty seconds of portentous guitar and drum interplay, the album detonates into existence as a squealing solo heralds

The White Stripes' first release on Sympathy for the Record Industry: 'The Big Three Killed My Baby'.

Meg and Jack, mean and moody, on the cover of their self-titled debut album.

'Jimmy The Exploder's' tonal descent into blues chaos. The thunderous blues riffage of the opening track catapults the listener through the down-home stomp of both sides of the new single, before the slide-propelled angst of 'Suzy Lee' arrests the album's breathless pace.

In addition to Jack's raw virtuosity and the Salvation Army-style tub-thumping provided by Meg, the album lays down the White Stripes' creative genetic code. Throughout the record, the duo's emphasis on simplicity is as ever-present as Jack's blues fundamentalism. Each song is underscored with a minimalist sensibility that has its roots in the mud of the Mississippi Delta. The album is dedicated to Son House, whose 'John The Revelator' segues into 'Cannon'.

Jack's lyrical fascination with the vagaries of human relationships is evident in 'Suzy Lee' (a song based around a schoolyard crush of Jack's, who later re-appears on 'We're Going To Be Friends'), 'Wasting My Time', 'One More Cup Of Coffee', and the contemplative 'Do'. It bears testament to Son House's assertion, 'ain't but one kind of blues and that consists of a male and female that's in love.'

The motif of childhood is represented by 'Little People', 'Sugar Never Tasted So Good' and 'Jimmy The Exploder' – a number about an imaginary monkey that, according to Jack, 'hates the colour blue and anything that is not red and has the power to explode those things with his mind.' Attempting to identify the roots of his fascination with childlike innocence and simplicity, Jack observed, 'sometimes I feel like it's an easy way for me to get honest. My love for the blues, and how I relate to it from where I'm from. I would feel really fake sitting down, adopting a black accent, and singing about trains or something. My easy way out of that is to just go into childhood, because that honesty seems to reflect the same nature that the blues was reflecting. That's my way of getting involved in that tradition.'

A key facet of *The White Stripes* is the way in which its inherent sparseness is manipulated to maximise the impact of sound, resonance and silence. As well as evoking the acoustic minimalism of early electric blues guitarists such as Howlin' Wolf and John Lee Hooker, Jack's fascination with sonics went beyond music and into the realm of science.

The guitarist is an ardent admirer of the physicist and inventor Nikolai Tesla, who is most famous for discovering the rotating magnetic field that forms the basis of most alternating current technologies. Tesla also experimented with resonance. 'He created a vibrating machine that could destroy a building with the right frequency,' explained Jack. 'But he also said that about the world as well: that if you simply found the right frequency and played it long enough, you could literally split the earth in half.'

Jack's fascination with the physicist led him to construct his own Tesla Coil – a high-frequency resonance transformer capable of producing tremendous voltage and spectacular electronic discharges. Additionally, the guitarist namechecks his hero on 'Astro' – a thunderous track with a nursery-rhyme lyric that was improvised over an instrumental

I hate the fact that the bluesman has been parodied – 'Oh, I woke up this morning and my baby's gone,' Blues Brothers kind of thing – when those guys are the gods of music. I mean, there should be statues of them everywhere. *Jack White*

at the recording sessions. 'The Astro is whatever you do in secret that nobody knows about,' revealed Jack. 'Everybody does the Astro. Jimmy [The Exploder] does the Astro.' Jack's Tesla Coil can be seen in *Coffee and Cigarettes*, a short film made by cult director Jim Jarmusch, in which the White Stripes appear as themselves.

However, any joy that Jack and Meg may have felt on finishing their debut album was undermined by the breakdown in their marital relationship. During the *White Stripes* sessions, the couple had agreed to break up. Meg moved out of Ferdinand Avenue in early February. As with all aspects of their private affairs, the duo have never spoken publicly about the reasons for their separation.

Irrespective of the background to the split, it's a testament to their creative focus that such a cohesive album was recorded under difficult emotional circumstances. Unsurprisingly, the future of the band was briefly in doubt – Meg was initially uncertain about continuing, forcing Jack to consider a replacement drummer ahead of the *Detroit Metro Times* Blowout Festival.

But, although by no means as musically obsessed as her newly estranged husband, Meg was thoroughly committed to the band. The dissolution of the Whites' relationship would, in fact, ultimately increase in the emotional intensity of their live performances.

'All music and art comes down to love,' observed Jack. 'It's depressing, because it feels like if love is true, and two people at one point can say how in love they are, and then one day one of them just decides, "No, I don't feel that way any more," and leaves, this person is left thinking, "Well, I still feel that way, I thought we both did." That's the oldest story in the book.'

Jack and Meg at the Detroit Metro Times' *'Blowout' festival.*

image can kill love

3

There's a thing that's being shoved down these twelve-year-old throats with these shows on MTV, like 'how to be a player,' and 'this is a mansion,' and Cribs, like 'look at my six cars out front.' It's teaching kids the wrong ideas about aspirations and life. I find it kind of sick. *Jack White*

A faithful representation of the duo's live set, *The White Stripes* was released by Sympathy for the Record Industry in June 1999. As with their earlier singles, the cover art corresponded to the red, white and black template. Its photographs were taken by Ko Shih (credited on the sleeve as 'Ko Melina Zydeko') – the bassist and frontwoman with Ko and the Knockouts, who would later become Meg's flatmate and go on to perform with the Dirtbombs.

Ko's cover shots depict an uncomfortable-looking duo, ill at ease with the artificiality of posing for a photograph. Several more candid images are to be found on the album's liner, which shows 1203 Ferdinand Avenue in all its red and white re-decorated splendour. Heather White's candy-cane motif is extended, both on the interior packaging and the disc itself. Further childhood references are provided by Jack's rambling liner notes, which allude to the uncertainty of young friendships and the lyrics of 'Jimmy The Exploder'.

Aware that the application of high-art ideals to rock 'n' roll would draw criticism, Jack insisted their concept was an integral aspect of the band: 'The idea of wearing just these colours, having just the two of us on stage – these are just boxes that we've cooked up to put ourselves in so that we can create better. If we had five people on the stage, all the opportunity of a 300-track studio, or a brand-new Les Paul, the creativity would be dead. Too much opportunity would make it too easy. We just don't want to be complicated, it seems unnecessary.'

Correspondingly, Jack felt there was no need to make use of the latest technology. 'Everybody these days wants to go into a fancy studio,' he explained, 'and record on a computer, and you have 74 amplifiers and all this digital equipment that's perfectly in

Boy and girl. Red and white. Brother and sister?

Meg demonstrates **Rolling Stone***'s assertion that 'you don't need bombast to make a blues explosion'.*

tune every time you play it. How stupid. It's like a friend of mine who's a painter was telling me, you go to an art supply store, and there's 700 different types of paint. That's kind of unfair: they should always sell you the primary colours, and you mix up your own.'

Contrasting with the guitar expertise demonstrated by Jack, Meg's rudimentary poundings played a key part in making the band's sound unique. Take away the drums and *The White Stripes* becomes just another alt-blues album by a talented solo artist. Meg's untutored technique connected her to this simplicity in a far more fundamental way than her virtuoso partner.

'I get jealous of Meg that way,' confessed Jack. 'I can be emotionally involved in the music too, but then that sort of male thing comes out of me where I have to figure out how it works, why it sounds good, why the guitar tone is interesting. I have to mechanically pick things apart sometimes.'

Meg's cherubic appearance and basic ability creates an impression of natural innocence, reinforcing the White Stripes' motif of uncomplicated infantilism. 'When we started, our objective was to be as simple as possible,' the guitarist explained. 'Meg's sound is like a little girl trying to play the drums and doing the best she can. Her playing on "The Big Three Killed My Baby" is the epitome of what I like about her drumming. It's just hits over and over again. It's not even a drumbeat – it's just accents.'

As well as being evocative of foot-stompin' blues, Jack recognised the importance of basic beat-keeping to the early sound of the Beatles and the Rolling Stones – 'Charlie Watts and Ringo, those guys got ribbed all the time because they weren't doing drum fills every two seconds. It's kind of stupid, especially once you get involved and realise how great Ringo and Charlie were and still are. I think they're amazing drummers.'

'Ringo knew what was needed,' agreed Meg, 'and he did what was right for the band, down to every little tiny thing needed for that song. And as much as I love all of the great drummers, there is that thing where it's about what the band needs. You know, when I hear music, I just hear the whole thing. I've never been much into picking things apart. It's the emotion of it that hits me, more than anything technical.'

With Goober and the Peas, Jack had experienced how a drummer can feel removed from a band's creative hub. Consequently, he was keen not to underplay the importance of Meg's role. 'When you've broken it down to just me and the drummer, it's still the drummer getting the short end of the stick. And then she gets ripped for not being [Rush drummer] Neil Peart or something. People miss the point. A lot of other guitar players that I liked started out being drummers, like Dick Dale. I think it's a smart thing, because you have that rhythm in your brain, so when you're writing music, that's a huge component of it.'

We're white people who play the blues, and our problem was how do we do that and not be fake? Our idea was to strip away everything unnecessary, to put ourselves in a box, to make rules for ourselves. *Jack White*

As with the inherent nostalgia of the blues, and the retrospective nature of evoking childhood, many of Jack's lyrics are suggestive of an earlier age. But still, any suggestion that the band are strip-mining the blues remains the surest way to annoy the normally placid guitarist: 'Someone once said that we were stealing from the old blues musicians, and making a profit from it. It was the most insulting thing I'd ever heard . . . We are trying to join a tradition of songwriting. The songs that we've covered – we've always paid the royalties to the people who wrote them if they weren't public domain. The biggest love in my life is blues music, so for someone to say that to me, I just wanted to punch them in the face.'

As a teenager he had written a poem entitled 'Image Can Kill Love'. 'It was anti things that had no meaning behind them, things that were done simply because they looked or sounded cool. Now it's just like everybody's got spiky hair and 50 piercings in their face', observed Jack. 'Is there any meaning behind it? A beef I have is image for the sake of image, cool for the sake of cool. If things don't have meaning behind it with you then all art falls apart at that point.'

This lack of substance is seen by the guitarist as endemic of the entire post-MTV generation. 'I don't want to be considered old-fashioned or a Luddite or conservative. But it's sad to see young kids today – they're sitting around listening to hip-hop or nu-metal, with a Sony PlayStation, a bong of marijuana. This is their life. It's a whole culture. And the parenting is so relaxed about that.'

Having identified the ethos of the modern era as directionless hedonism, Jack's self-imposed limitations were aimed at preventing any such self-indulgence. In addition to rejecting extraneous musical elements, the red, white and black dress code was intended to downplay, rather than reinforce, any accent on image. 'Like a uniform at school,' offers Meg, 'you can just focus on what you're doing because everybody's wearing the same thing.' Interestingly, given the break-up of their marriage, Jack saw the stagewear as emblematic of the White Stripes' unity: 'When we're doing something with the band, it's another way to keep us together, to keep us solid as a unit.'

Jack White's mildly fogeyish disdain for the ill discipline of today's youth, and his insistence on politeness, corresponds to his emphasis on personal discipline. 'If you were touring the house of some old famous person,' he reflected, 'and he never liked any light bulbs in the house, and he only lit the house by candle – people are so enthused by that. "Oh, that's interesting that he had these rules." It makes you feel like this guy lived by certain notions that propelled him to be happy and to create. I like that idea. It at least symbolises that that person is working toward something.'

Given that Jack rarely drinks, is vehemently drug-free and shows no desire to squire groupies, it would be appealing to view him as some kind of puritanical killjoy. But, essentially, Jack believes that there is a correct time and place for flamboyance and wilfulness. 'When we played we decided we wanted to dress up in our Sunday best like a kid would . . . If you tell a kid that they are going to church, they'll always come down in a red outfit or something and be told; "No, you can't go to church in that."'

Despite the rejection of 'image', the separation of performance from mundane everyday activity is in keeping with Jack's rigid sense of order. 'We wanted to present ourselves in some way. Everybody wears street clothes all the time. Why should we just do that? Blues musicians that are my idols, they wore their nicest suits and nicest hats when they played shows. It's just being polite. It's like going to church. You wouldn't wear your pyjamas to church.'

Once onstage, whatever apparel a performer chooses to wear becomes, inescapably, their 'image'. 'We could go out and play in our street clothes under the [pretext] that we're "being real", but you know, it's still an image,' remarked Jack.

The choice of a red, black and white colour scheme – in preference to the yellow, black and white of Third Man Upholstery – was based on the fact that red is far more eye-catching than yellow. 'It's just more powerful,' announced Jack. 'For some reason, it just makes people think about stuff. Say someone says, "Wow, I really like your red pants." It just seems to me that if I was wearing green pants, people wouldn't come up and say, "Wow, those are pants." There's nothing special about them. They're just old senior citizen pants. There's just something about the colour.'

The White Stripes' manifesto of creative self-limitation extended to their live shows. In order to maintain integrity and focus, the duo avoided set lists – preferring to let the selection of songs be determined by the atmosphere. Being a duo, it was far easier to take

Meg and Jack: 'The telepathy of Siamese twins.'

The songs just magically appear. Sometimes at sound checks they'll suddenly appear out of nowhere – or usually in the middle of a show. *Meg White*

such an improvisational approach than would have been the case in a larger group. The close relationship between Jack and Meg established an intuitive understanding that ensured embarrassing gaps between numbers were largely avoided.

'It's the best thing,' Jack enthused, 'that communication we've developed on stage. We can read each other's mind, and really make each show different from the last. We started off using a set list in the beginning, but I would just end up ignoring it.'

'That was worse,' recalled Meg. 'I'd look up and go, "we're gonna play this next . . . Oh no, we're not!" Now I can usually tell if he plays a certain song a certain way what he's going to play next.'

'That's one of the great things about the White Stripes,' insisted Dan Miller, 'because he can change keys in a song. He and Meg are locked in. From early on, they had that down.'

The idea of ensuring that each performance was unique appealed to Jack's sense of creative honesty, as well as evoking the spontaneity of his blues idols. 'You could go to see a glam rock band and say, "This is really exciting," but that's far from honesty. If a musician listens to Charley Patton and doesn't hear anything at all, I don't think they should call themselves musicians, because they're obviously just looking for fun and kicks and a good time out of it.'

For Jack, hedonistic pleasure was inconsistent with his fundamentalist view of music's importance, particularly the blues. 'They should teach it in school,' he asserted. 'Country, and rock and roll, and punk, and everything else, it's all the blues. But the blues is the purest form of it. It's the pinnacle of a mountain that slopes down into other types of music.'

Jack's preoccupation with honesty pervades every aspect of the White Stripes – the minimalism of the band's sound, the stripping away of all unnecessary embellishment, and the conceptualisation of childhood, simplicity and discipline are all driven by a need for creative integrity. The idea that any music stemming from raw emotion is imbued with similar honesty allows a variety of genres to be incorporated into the band's sonic patchwork. This has come to include country, folk, garage, old show tunes and punk rock.

However, in terms of Jack White's stylistic hierarchy, it is the blues that have come to epitomise this purity. 'It's so truthful, it can't be glamorised. If people really love music, they're going to start being drawn toward honesty, and if they're drawn to that, it's a direct line right back to Charley Patton and Son House. I'm very sceptical of musicians who say they love music and don't love the blues. It's like someone saying they don't like the Beatles: It makes you think they're in it for the wrong ideas.'

Despite being a blues zealot, Jack recognised the way that old music can be perceived as inaccessible. 'It's hard for a lot of people to get interested in it, because blues just seems like an old-time photo of your mom or something. You see a 1940s movie and say, "That lady is really pretty," and then someone else will say, "Oh, she looks like an old lady." But she's probably twenty in the film.'

Similarly, the origin of the blues lies in the suffering of a black minority subjected to relentless exploitation and oppression. Correspondingly, it's become viewed as a primarily old-school black phenomenon, far easier for white audiences to connect with in its variant forms. Or for white performers to pastiche what they consider to be wild, bluesy antics.

As Jack avers, 'I wish music could be more like Cole Porter and different Broadway writers from back in the thirties and forties – more melody and idea instead of just chords and lamenting about girls and cars or drugs. That's really getting old. I think that song structures of the twenties and thirties were so accessible to people. Melody was so important. Not that it isn't in pop music today, but it was on a more basic, simple level back then.'

Most forms of modern popular music are rooted in the chord and verse structures of the blues, which have been diluted and adapted to appeal to the audiences of the day. As proto-punk and blues enthusiast Richard Hell describes, 'The progression took place over a span of only about 60 years, and though at each stage the music became a little less local and eccentric, it's all blues, until it disperses into a kind of loamy "pop" that the blues (and other folk music) made possible. Like the Stones, Dylan and Prince.'

As is the case with the Rolling Stones, the White Stripes' blues influences are exceptionally direct – just as Mick Jagger's vocal delivery mimicked the accents of Muddy Waters or Howlin' Wolf, Jack White's arrangements and guitar chops evoke the Delta bluesmen of an earlier era. As Hell later remarked, 'I'd figured that this dispersion was where the tradition became so diluted as to be thought of as played out and finished, but check the White Stripes now.'

A rigid adherent to twelve-bar blues fundamentalism, Jack declared, 'The moment when that progression was accomplished in the early part of the twentieth century was the most perfect moment in songwriting of all time. There's something about that that's so easily understandable, that repeating line. It translates to the next person so easily. Which is what song writing is supposed to do: translating an idea, communicating an idea through melody and storytelling and rhythm.'

A blues song is simple and raw, and it's not polished, but it's perfect because it's based off a simple idea. *Jack White*

The commonly-portrayed lifestyle of the down-home Southern bluesman can seem at odds with Jack's self-imposed abstemiousness. Inhabiting a harsh and often violent world of forced labour, itinerant poverty and perpetual uncertainty, the early blues musicians were often inclined toward heroic alcohol consumption and rampant whoremongering. Recognising the gulf between such indulgences and his own strict morals, Jack explains, 'these are my idols, yet I probably disagree with their lifestyle a lot: wife beating, drinking and carousing, sick behaviour like that. I'm respecting the notions they're conveying in their music but I'm not really respecting the people they are. But Michelangelo was probably a complete egomaniac jerk, too, y'know?'

As was the case with 'Let's Shake Hands', the White Stripes' parochial profile limited the impact of their debut album – a small band, on a small label with a negligible publicity budget.

Those close to the band were delighted with the record. 'The first album was really a document of what the band was like, their live show,' Dan Miller affirmed. 'Jim Diamond did a good job of capturing the power. Lyrically, it was such an amazing thing listening to it for the first time. For a lot of people who'd seen the band live, with crappy PA's and all, you couldn't really make out the poetry, the Dylanesque aspect of Jack's lyrics.'

Jack and Meg strike a familial pose for the media.

Acclaim from afar came via Corey Brown's *San Francisco Bay Guardian* review: 'The White Stripes are rock and roll's second chance to rebel properly, picking up the torch the very moment it was dropped, this time with both finesse and abandon, a reverb-laden twist of divine providence realised by a young man who plays criminally charming electric licks and sings with a striking wail and his little sister who lays the rhythm thicklike.'

Well, we're brother and sister of course. *Jack White*

The idea of Meg as Jack's 'little sister' is the impish mechanism the separated couple adopted to deflect media questions about their private lives. But their ersatz sibling status was reinforced by Jack's regular onstage references to his 'big sister'. (Clearly, the age difference between brother and sister was one angle they hadn't got straight.)

What had started as an in-joke soon gained its own momentum. The physical similarities between the duo and their instinctive musical syncopation only served to validate the jape. 'We've heard that ever since we started,' chuckled Jack. 'I don't know what it is. Some people come up to us and say, "God, you guys really look like you're brother and sister." And we say, "That's because we are!"'

The idea of a pair of siblings from a large Catholic family chimed directly with the duo's other emblems of innocence. It was quickly adopted as a means of self-mythologising – exactly the sort of down-home, poor-but-happy image that would appeal to Jack's sensibilities and provide evidence of sense of devilment in Meg.

When the band later gained momentum, the familial myth gave the media a hook to hang them on. Taken as rote by unwary researchers, the falsehood was rehashed and repeated until almost every piece written about the White Stripes contained the phrase, 'Detroit brother-and-sister combo . . .'

As the truth later leaked out via web postings of the couple's marriage and divorce certificates, intense speculation was generated – to which Jack and Meg responded with customary evasion. *Time* magazine joined the stampede and published an 'expose' revealing the truth about the Whites' marriage. It was a source of some mirth for those in Detroit who already knew the truth and were party to the brother and sister charade.

Jack obviously didn't care whether the shallow-minded were confused by all the obfuscation. 'If you look at the White Stripes from a distance,' he declared, 'somebody who didn't really want to dig deep into us would say that we were super-gimmicky. "They dress in these colours, and they're a boy and a girl, and they're brother and sister, but people think they're really married." . . . . It's perfect for us, because it weeds out all the people who don't really love the honesty of music.'

As well as playing a successful series of smaller local shows, the White Stripes promoted their debut album before larger audiences during their first major tour as a support act. Added to a bill headlined by indie darlings Pavement and the Ramones-influenced 'Riot Grrls' Sleater Kinney, Jack and Meg were suddenly pushed out on stage to open in front of audiences of up to 2,000 people.

Somewhat taken aback, Jack and Meg's nervousness and dislike of playing for big crowds imbued their set with Ramonic velocity. 'When they toured with Pavement in September or October of 1999, I had this great soundboard tape of this show,' recalled Ben Blackwell. 'There were 800 people there, by far the biggest crowd they had ever played in front of. They were supposed to play a half-hour set or something, but because they were so nervous they played it super fast and did it in twenty minutes. There was this amazing solo on "Let's Shake Hands".'

The duo's unease was typical of the traditional reluctance of Detroit bands to break out of their self-contained local circuit. Such a reluctance to leave home turf meant that bands such as the Hentchmen failed to reach audiences who would have catapulted them to national recognition. Keen to ensure the White Stripes escaped the dwarf-star pull of Detroit, Long Gone John stressed the importance of getting out on the road: 'The missing element with these bands, or any band, is touring.'

The immense reservoir of material that Jack had accrued enabled the band to begin work on their second album almost as soon as *The White Stripes* hit the shops. Although the new record was once again mixed by Jim Diamond at Ghetto, the taping sessions took place at Third Man Studios and were produced by Jack. 'We didn't want to make the same album twice, even though the first album went over really well,' he explained. 'We didn't want to try to repeat it. So we recorded the whole second album in my living room. There wasn't any studio influence, so we felt comfortable, and Meg felt comfortable.'

It minimised the band's customarily miserly recording costs (a paltry $600 for Jim Diamond's mixing), but recording an album in his front room did entail one unforeseen problem. Aside from constant interruptions by the telephone and sundry visitors, a local drunk walked in off of the street during the recording of 'Death Letter'. 'He'd just wandered by because he'd heard us playing,' recalled Jack.

As with *The White Stripes*, the instrumental augmentation on the new LP was kept to a minimum. Aside from John Szymanski's harmonica on 'Hello Operator', the only other additional musician was Paul Henry Ossy – who contributes violin to 'I'm Bound To Pack It Up' and 'Why Can't You Be Nicer To Me?'.

However, so ingrained was Jack's commitment to 'breaking things down' that he felt it necessary to justify even this low level of embellishment. 'On this album, we have overdubbed piano and acoustic guitar, just feeling out the differences between us playing live and recording a really good song. We get that all the time – "You can't reproduce that on stage." Nobody cares when there's four people in the band, and they can't play piano on stage either. With two pieces, people are like, "You can't play that live." Neither could the Beatles.'

Indeed, such was Jack's zeal for minimalism that he later admitted to regrets about overdubbing some piano and acoustic guitar. 'I think that was too much. Now listening, it's too much. I guess I was testing the water, seeing how much we could build this up.'

To underline the White Stripes' preoccupation with simplicity and reductionism, Jack invoked his primary art influence. 'I thought we'd call the album *De Stijl* because it broke the art form down to the simplest parts, and they had to abandon it because they couldn't get it any simpler than it was. It was a question of how simple should the White Stripes be, what's out of bounds for us, and what are we supposed to be doing with this band?'

The first LP's really angry, you know. This LP we tried to get a little cleaner. Maybe we changed from anger to bitterness. *Jack White*

Musically, the disc can be viewed as a refinement of the explosive blues-rock that comprised its predecessor. Certainly, *De Stijl* is far less raw than *The White Stripes*, with a clearer mix and a softening of Jack's furious guitar assault and vocal delivery combining with a greater emphasis on arrangement to produce a gentler overall sound.

'So that was the challenge for us' declared Jack, 'how simple can this band be and still be melodic and still be something people can listen to and feel something?' With the duo's more explosive ingredients subsumed in the name of simplicity, it was hoped that the emotional impact of the songs would come to the fore. Jack believed the reduction in volume would evoke the subtle impact of simple acoustic blues and folk music.

'It might sound stupid, but they all have this feeling to them. That has power behind it. Not necessarily loud, electric power, it could even be a slow blues song or a Broadway tune, even something like Dylan lyrics can have so much power behind them, and they can be so quiet. That's what we strive to achieve.'

Jack's subtler vocal delivery was a partial reaction to comparisons with other vocalists, such as Led Zeppelin's white blues cockrocker Robert Plant. 'The new LP has a lot more low singing on it but it's like, no matter what I do, someone will say I sound like this or that. If there was something that existed like a completely original band that played, people at the show would be dying to compare it to something like Devo or whatever. People have tried this before. People have tried to mimic the blues with hard, loud equipment.'

I listened to a lot of Blind Willie McTell while making this record. We do that McTell song at the end of the record that Meg also sang on. It was the first time Meg sang on any of our records, so that was fun. *Jack White*

Of the thirteen tracks included on *De Stijl*, eleven are original compositions; with the two cover versions being Son House's 'Death Letter' (the track that launched Jack's blues obsession) and a version of 'Your Southern Can Is Mine', which was originally by another legendary bluesman, Blind Willie McTell. Along with Son House and Robert Johnson, McTell completes Jack's personal trinity of blues influences, and the album is dedicated to him – alongside Gerrit Rietveld.

Born in Georgia during 1901, Willie Samuel McTell developed a unique fingerpicking guitar style that lent itself to a diverse range of genres, including blues, ragtime and folk. His reserved vocal style and articulate lyricism is a distinct influence on the approach adopted by Jack White for *De Stijl*.

Like many of the legendary blues guitarists of the 1920s and thirties, McTell's musical legacy was far more substantial than his own commercial success. In order to avoid onerous contractual obligations, Blind Willie recorded under a plethora of pseudonyms (a partial selection includes Barrelhouse Sammy, Blind Doogie, Blind Sammy, Blind Sammie, Blind Willie, Georgia Bill, Red Hot Willie Glaze, Hot Shot Willie and Pig 'n' Whistle Red).

Although much of his life was spent hoboing from one town to the next, often playing for spare change on street corners, McTell continued to record well into his fifties. His final sessions came in 1956, three years before his death. 'He was still playing on supermarkets and street corners in the late fifties,' explained Jack. 'It makes me jealous to think that my father – if he'd been a blues lover then – could have gone down to Georgia and seen him play in front of a Piggly-Wiggly [self-service grocery store].'

The Mondrian-influenced cover of the White Stripes'
second album, De Stijl.

Posthumously McTell returned to prominence during the revival in interest in the blues during the early 1960's. One of his foremost admirers was Bob Dylan, who wrote an eponymous homage to the legendary guitarist in 1983. Paying tribute to McTell's influence, Jack observed, 'I think people have heard the name, but he seems to be really overlooked. He knew a lot about melody, and how melody is so important to a song structure. I don't understand why his songs aren't famous, like "God Bless America".'

From the opening chords of the album's first track, the poppy 'You're Pretty Good Looking For A Girl', Jack's use of McTell-inspired restraint is evident. *De Stijl* features no guitar

We had wondered how simple we could get things before we would have to build it back up again. How simple we could get with people still liking what we do. *Jack White*

solos, and songs such as 'Death Letter' and the future set-opener 'Sister, Do You Know My Name' reach a climax without Jack needing to cut loose. However, although the track is partially redeemed by Jack's expert guitar picking, the concentration on subtlety at the expense of velocity is over-indulged on the plodding 'A Boy's Best Friend'.

The White Stripes' fascination with childhood is most evident in 'Apple Blossom', a pretty slice of acoustic folk that was later recorded by a nursery school teacher with her class, who sent a videotape of the performance to the band. 'I started crying,' revealed Jack. 'This teacher, she played songs for her kids and she taught them this song. It's really great, I thought. You can't top that. If it's gotten to that, how can you top that?'

Further extension of the childhood motif on *De Stijl* comes in the form of a young boy's spoken introduction to 'Let's Build A Home', a track where restraint is momentarily consumed by raw energy. This frantic blast of blues-punk sees the duo thrashing and whooping deep into psychobilly territory, with Jack's vocals reminiscent of the Cramps' Lux Interior. Further obvious garage-band influences include the Sonics on the stomping 'Jumble Jumble'.

As it was on *The White Stripes*, Jack's lyrical preoccupation with romantic angst is revisited several times on *De Stijl*. The evocations of isolated longing work well enough on 'Truth Doesn't Make A Noise' and 'Why Can't You Be Nicer To Me'. However, 'I'm Bound To Pack It Up' is an overly sweet acoustic number that provides the album's low point. Interestingly, it's also the one song where Meg's contribution is reduced to practically nil.

De Stijl is a far less consistent body of work than its predecessor. The move away from the visceral abandon of *The White Stripes* toward softer material produces an unevenness. The album's outstanding track is 'Little Bird', a soaring miasma of tremolo-laden slide guitar that ends up somewhere deep in the Southern Chitlin Circuit.

I was really into furniture design . . . and I liked Gerrit Rietveld – he did a red-blue chair for De Stijl. And it really had meaning to me and to the band and the music and the aesthetic of our live performance. *Jack White*

The Blind Willie McTell cover, 'Your Southern Can Is Mine', represents the pre-electric, down-home blues style, and is notable for Meg's debut on backing vocals. Nominated to be the first single taken from *De Stijl*, 'Hello Operator' showcases the hysterical urgency of Jack's vocals to magnificent effect. Lyrically, the song re-visits the anti-corporate theme of 'The Big Three Killed My Baby'. 'That's a phone company finger-pointing song,' asserted Jack. 'I hate the rip-off company. I know everyone has to have a job, everyone has to work and get a pay check to keep everything going, but it's pathetic that the better mouse trap doesn't win out.'

In a break with the tradition of keeping sleeve design in-house, the packaging for the new LP featured a series of images in *De Stijl*, which were photographed by occasional Dirtbombs drummer Ewolf (Eric Wheeler). The essential trinity of colours was maintained, with the cover depicting a white-clad Jack and Meg surrounded by Mondrian inspired blocks of red, white and black.

Written by Jack, the liner notes are a reductivist mission statement: 'When ideas become too complicated, and the pursuit of perfection is misconstrued as a need for excess. When there is so much involved that individual components cannot be discerned. When it is hard to break the rules of excess, then new rules need to be established. It descends back to the beginning where the construction of things visual or aural is too uncomplicated not to be beautiful. But this is done in the knowledge that we can only become simple to a point and then there is nowhere else to go. There are definite natural things that cannot be broken down into lesser components. Even if the goal of achieving beauty from simplicity is aesthetically less exciting it may force the mind to acknowledge the simple components that make the complicated beautiful.' The album is co-dedicated to Gerrit Rietveld, whose work Jack had initially encountered while studying furniture design.

One key difference between artists such as Rietveld and Mondrian and the early bluesmen was that the former practiced limitation through choice – whereas the latter had it forced upon them by poverty.

For the White Stripes, it was a personal notion of discipline. 'We always wear red and white at our shows,' explained Jack. 'It's kind of like our "colours". We always do everything that way to kind of keep order. And that philosophy is reflected in the De Stijl movement.'

> **Someone will say, 'Hey why not cause a storm by wearing green one day?' I mean, why? Why would we do that? Wearing red and white has meaning. Wearing green for a day would just be so bourgeois.** *Jack White*

While the guitarist saw discipline as a safeguard against pretentious self-indulgence, however, he later conceded that an over-emphasis on simplicity could itself be self-indulgent. 'When we're writing songs, sometimes it gets too simple. There's nothing there to hold onto. But it's a 50/50 thing. You should try to be playing for other people as well as just doing it for yourself.'

Jack applied similar logic to the question of whether a defined visual image was counter to his minimalist ideal: 'there is a visual aspect to a show. People are watching. You could compare that with the way we wear white and red peppermint candy as a symbol of the band . . . if we had to make a choice, I wanted it to be something simple like that. Something where someone could see a cover and say, "oh, that's a White Stripes record" right away. I mean, I won't go dressing up as a chicken just to get people's attention.'

Once more, Sympathy for the Record Industry opted to issue a single ahead of the album's June 2000 release. As one of the standout cuts from the LP, 'Hello

'Hello Operator'/'Jolene' (Sympathy for the Record Industry, 2000).

Operator' was duly selected. Although later described by the *NME* as 'a two-minute 36 second encapsulation of everything that [blues revivalist] Jon Spencer had been trying to achieve for over a decade', it was the B-side – a cover of Dolly Parton's 'Jolene' – that attracted most of the attention.

An incongruous choice of song for a 'hip' band to cover in a reverential and non-ironic manner, the White Stripes' spare unfussiness builds to a thunderous climax, with Jack's voice imbuing the Nashville standard with new emotional intensity. Nominating 'Jolene' as 'one of the greatest country songs ever written', Jack saw recording the live favourite as a means of paying tribute. 'Both me and Meg always loved that song. It's in a minor key and almost has an evil tone to it,' he explained. 'We've always loved country music. We wanted to do a country single with Dolly on one side and Loretta on the other. I first heard Dolly Parton a couple years ago, and couldn't believe what a good thing she had going at one point.'

In terms of sales, the new single was always unlikely to break out of the lower independent league. But 'Hello Operator/Jolene' added to the growing local interest in the band. One show at a jam-packed Gold Dollar was attended by a far wider demographic than the regular Detroit indie hardcore. Additionally, the media reaction to *De Stijl* was no longer confined to the Detroit press and garage rock fan sites.

I'd be concerned if anyone met us and didn't get the feeling, 'What a polite young band.' *Jack White*

Writing in *Rolling Stone*, Jenny Eclisu introduced the duo's stripped-down sound to a wider public: 'White's knack for phrasing – both his vocals and guitar lines – gives the songs the feel of improvisation. And Meg White's drumming is so minimal that it's almost funny: It forces a smile because, like everything about the White Stripes, it proves that you don't need bombast to make a blues explosion.'

Closer to home, in the *Detroit Metro Times*, Chris Handyside introduced the band as 'a man-woman duo with an aggressively ambiguous relationship, a penchant for nursery-rhyme simplicity masking deep, dark secrets, and sporting trademark red-and-white garb.' Describing *De Stijl* as 'fucking brilliant', Handyside asserted, 'You'd have to be truly sick not to relate at least a little to Jack White's insights, declarations of insecurity and boy-next-door-with-the-crooked-grin vocalisations.'

Further praise was forthcoming from Dan Miller, who saw the band steadily improving. 'With *De Stijl*, you saw better fidelity with the recording, but some of the stuff Jack just recorded in his living room. I think you saw more of the progression – developing songs and messing with the arrangements more, more of a pop aspect.'

Although the critical praise for *De Stijl* far outweighed the album's commercial impact, the response to the disc was sufficient to enable the White Stripes to land a series of high-profile support slots. These included a sold-out Los Angeles date with Weezer and a further tour with Sleater-Kinney that would take in the East Coast, Midwest and Canada. Locally, the band's growing popularity meant that shows at the intimate Gold Dollar were likely to leave many more disappointed punters outside the venue than would actually manage to squeeze in.

Offering 'Billiards, Bands and Beverages', the Magic Stick is the self-proclaimed 'home of rock in Detroit'. Larger than the Gold Dollar, the venue enabled the White Stripes to accommodate a greater proportion of the hometown crowd. Greg Baise, the venue's promotions director, had followed Jack and Meg's progress since their earliest shows, and was only too pleased to book them. 'These are people who not only create music but listen to music closely,' enthused Baise. 'There's a lot of work that goes into it, which is kind of deceptive, because people might look at it and go, "Oh, it's just a drummer and a guitarist." But there's a lot more to it than that. Jack's a great lyricist, and great at paying homage to his antecedents and things he's interested in.'

With a series of low-key dates in New Zealand, Australia and Japan mooted for the end of 2000, Jack decided to abandon Third Man Upholstery and concentrate on the band as a full-time occupation. Quitting the day job came as a relief for Jack, who, given his distaste for the financial side of the trade, seemed to be permanently struggling to keep his business afloat.

'I was broke all the time,' he recalled. Like many traditional trades, the upholstery business faced a perpetually declining market, due largely to the ready availability of cheap, mass-produced, pre-fabricated furniture. Despite the years of on-the-job training required to become a master of the craft, Jack's choice of music over upholstery was not a difficult decision. 'I was having a lot of trouble,' he insisted, 'and I would talk to these guys when I went to pick up supplies. I asked how long they thought it would take me before I could whip out a chair really fast and start making better money . . . . They told me it was probably going to take me between eight and ten years before I'd be really comfortable. I was like, "Ah, man, I just can't do it."'

With his upholsterer's equipment stored away at Ferdinand Avenue, Jack soon found the band taking up much of the time he previously allocated to his trade. Having neither a publicist nor an agent, the guitarist had to devote a lot of energy to the administrative aspects of the band. 'He's on the phone, literally, the entire day. And we got two phone lines and one's going off, and then the other one,' described Meg.

'Not like it's bragging or anything, but it kind of takes away from the fact that it's nice to not have a job and be a musician,' Jack observed. 'People say, "Oh, God, why are you complaining about all that?" But it does get annoying.'

Ahead of the Sleater-Kinney tour, the White Stripes headed out on the road under their own steam. Despite Jack undergoing a brief hospitalisation caused by a troublesome kidney stone (an incident which followed hot on the heels of his nearly being trampled by an excitable North Dakotan buffalo), the duo were swiftly coming to terms with some of the less exciting elements of life on the road.

'It's hard, because Meg doesn't like to joke around much,' revealed a glum Jack. 'I like to all the time so there's that. We read, listen to music. We just got a CD thing for the van. We brought something like 200 CDs with us. We listen to music a lot. I write.'

With the duo now locked into the familiar tour-album-tour cycle, their stage set became ever more tightly honed. The constant gigging improved Meg's power and confidence, and the duo often seemed to communicate on stage with sub-telepathic nods and shrugs. As the White Stripes grew into their newfound status of minor indie rock stars, critical and audience reaction became increasingly positive.

'I guess we started getting more attention once we got to open for Sleater-Kinney and go on a tour with them,' remarked Jack. 'We got into a bigger audience. People who worked for the press or record labels would go to those shows. We were putting on a pretty good show by that point, I guess, so it was good timing.'

Greg Baise recalled the duo's rising popularity: 'I remember each show getting more and more packed. It usually takes a lot to sell out the Magic Stick. Like a New Year's Eve gig or something like that. It's very rare that even the best local bands sell that place out, but they did that several times.'

Buoyed by the increasing attention, the White Stripes spent the late autumn touring the Pacific Rim, undertaking a series of shows at bars and small clubs. Although their recorded output was only available on import outside of the USA and Europe, the gigs were fairly well-attended.

They went on tour with Sleater-Kinney and the next thing anybody knew they were famous. *Mick Collins*

Jack, however, confessed to a small degree of culture shock upon encountering his first Japanese audience. 'It was kind of a weird reaction. The crowd wouldn't clap after songs – I don't know why. People would come up after the show and say that they really liked it though.'

Despite the low-budget, whistle-stop nature of the tour, the shows played a vital role in establishing the band in Australia and New Zealand – where they would later return to play sold-out gigs at much larger venues and enjoy Top 40 chart successes. To help promote the band in the Pacific territories, the White Stripes' version of Blind Willie McTell's 'Lord Send Me An Angel' was pressed up as a single. Backed by 'You're Pretty Good Looking (Trendy American Remix)', the 45 was subsequently re-issued in the US by Sympathy for the Record Industry.

Once again produced by Jack and mixed at Ghetto Recorders, the re-issue was pressed in limited numbers and came in a paper wraparound sleeve featuring a similar image to the cover of *De Stijl*. Further recordings quickly followed in the form of three Captain Beefheart covers for a limited edition, seven-inch Sub Pop Singles Club release: 'Party Of Special Things To Do', backed with 'China Pig' and 'Ashtray Heart'. The White Stripes also contributed a new track, 'Handsprings', to a single given away free

Jack at the Magic Stick, during the De Stijl *launch concert in June 2000.*

with issue nineteen of pinball magazine *Multiball*. (The flip side featured the Dirtbombs' 'Cedar Point'.) Recounting, in spoken-word form, the perils of taking a date to a hustler-infested bowling alley, 'Handsprings' later appeared on a pinball-themed compilation album, *Hot Pinball Rock*, issued by Extra Ball Records.

As the year drew to a close, the White Stripes' hectic schedule showed little sign of slowing down. Preparations were being made for their third album; with so much new material added to Jack's stash of as-yet-unused songs, the possibility of a double LP was given serious consideration. The positive response to *De Stijl* and the tour with Sleater-Kinney also meant a national headline tour was a viable proposition.

Even if we did become MTV material, it's not gonna change what we do. *Jack White*

Recording sessions for the album were scheduled for February 2001. The increase in the White Stripes' creative stock also attracted rumours of major-label interest. This made little impression on Jack, who announced he was perfectly happy where he was: '[Long Gone John has] helped us along the way so long. Other labels like Sub Pop or whatever, have gotten success with things, gotten lucky. I don't know if Sympathy's ever had a band that's been really huge or anything. So if it does happen, if it gets bigger, it would be nice to be on a label like that . . . When you get into all that money and people telling you what to do, it's just harassment.'

Altogether more welcome attention came when the White Stripes were named as one of *Rolling Stone*'s ten bands to watch for 2001. Given that their publicity machine consisted of little more than Jack and a booking agent, it was something of a coup. Jack was delighted with the nomination. 'It feels honest you know? It doesn't feel like we got into *Rolling Stone* because someone had a favour or sent them a ton of CD's.'

a bigger room

We've created our own little world. When you do that, nothing can get you. *Meg White*

4

Jack White began the New Year in Third Man Studios (that is, in his own living room), compiling and producing tracks for a Detroit-themed compilation album – *Sympathetic Sounds Of Detroit*. Essentially a sampler for bands on Sympathy for the Record Industry, the LP revealed the extent of talent on the local scene. In addition to local heavyweights such as the Dirtbombs, the Detroit Cobras, Bantam Rooster and the Hentchmen, the album also featured newer bands like the Soledad Brothers and the Von Bondies.

'We did the entire thing at my house, on the same mikes and the same amps, so it has that consistency to it,' recalled Jack. 'Everyone brought an original song. I'm so happy. I thought everyone was going to bring a bunch of crap, but they all came with the goods.'

As well as recording and producing the album, Jack got together with Meg to contribute 'Red Death At 6:14', a stop-start exercise in suffocating urgency. The song, later issued as a free single with *Mojo*, was accompanied by a 22-second track entitled 'Buzzard Blues'.

Sympathetic Sounds condensed the Detroit scene, featuring a selection of groups who had regularly swapped personnel and gigged together. Chris Handyside, the former music editor of the *Detroit Metro Times* experienced this cross-fertilisation at firsthand during his tenure with the Dirtbombs and the Hentchmen: 'There's totally a romanticized view of Detroit,' he asserted. 'The reality of Detroit, though, is very barren and very self-sufficient.'

Separated from the New York-Los Angeles coastal music scenes both culturally and geographically, Detroit's musicians tended to operate within their own enclosed boundaries. Handyside explained, 'You cling to who you find, so things heat up rather fast in terms of groups of people working together. There's also a lot of boredom, and there's a lot of living low to the ground.'

The close-knit nature of the scene is evident on *Sympathetic Sounds*. In addition to stalwarts like Mick Collins and Jon Szymanski, the album features contributions from other musicians who had close ties with the White Stripes: Ben Swank of the Soledad Brothers, who had moved in with Jack subsequent to his break up with Meg, and Ko Shih (of Ko and the Knockouts), who was now Meg's flatmate.

To further entangle the web of relationships within the Detroit garage clan, the Von Bondies' Marcie Bolen had recently become Jack's girlfriend. 'It's an incestuous scene, sometimes painfully so,' observed Handyside.

Despite the quantity of talent within the local rock scene, Detroit's rock acts rarely

Jack and Meg, in a studio portrait, January 2002.

The Von Bondies: Don Blum, Marcie Bolen, Carrie Smith, Jason Stollsteimer.

attracted interest from major labels. While rap and R&B-influenced natives like Eminem, Kid Rock and Aaliyah were catapulted to international stardom, the likes of the Gories and the Hentchmen were entrenched firmly at home.

This sense of isolation was reflected in Jack's liner notes for *Sympathetic Sounds*: 'Detroit's musicians don't suffer from the anxiety of not getting signed or not having a connection to get their music in a film. We know from the beginning that it's never gonna happen. No suit from L.A. or New York is gonna fly to Detroit to check out a band and hand out business cards.'

Although subsequent events were to prove Jack to be spectacularly wrong, at the time there was a complete dearth of A&R people hanging around the Gold Dollar or Magic Stick. 'I think Jack was really sincere when he wrote that, because it was really like that,' offered Dan Miller. ' "I'm gonna record all of them using the same drum kit, the same amps, in my house, and who cares? Hopefully this might be interesting for a few hundred people, and it'll be something to capture a moment in time." And you wouldn't think that a lot of people would care about that.'

As photographer and Dirtbombs drummer Pat Pantano explained, even the scene's elder statesmen were living life in the bus lane: 'People ask about Mick Collins a lot . . . They're like, "Is he a star and running all over the country?" It's like, "No, the motherfucker don't even got a car! What are you talking about?"'

As a body of work, *Sympathetic Sounds* paints an authentic picture of a Detroit scene that was shortly to become the focus of music press attention in the same way that Seattle had ten years earlier. Owing much to the driving influence of 1960s garage bands such as the Sonics and ? and the Mysterians, the record provided Jack with an opportunity to show his affection for the genre.

Having highlighted his love of the blues on the first two White Stripes LPs, though, the guitarist would turn to country music as inspiration for the band's third full-length release. 'We'd like it to be a double album, 'cause there's enough material. I'm thinking about doing one disc at a real studio and one disc here at home. Just a bunch of country songs and a lot of piano songs that I've written.'

People have made this big deal about Detroit having a history of the way bands present themselves visually, the rawness and emotion of the music, and that's something Jack's always been all about – having that real emotion come through. Sometimes it's a little bit deceptive, intentionally – there's a little bit of irony. *Dan Miller*

The idea of dividing the recording sessions between sites suggested how Jack was not entirely convinced of his studio skills. 'I'm not very good at recording,' he admitted. 'I don't know where to put mikes; I don't know what the right frequencies are for things. I just try to do what sounds right.'

Ultimately it was decided that the new album would be recorded at Easley-McCain studios in Memphis. Initial suggestions that studio owner Doug McCain (who had previously produced Pavement and the Breeders) would be involved quickly came to nothing as Jack decided to produce the record himself, with mixing assistance from Stewart Sikes.

'Some bands can write amazing songs but they don't know how to record them, so they have to have a producer,' explained Jack. 'But if we can keep everything in this big box and keep people away from us, at least we can be proud of it. Like, if someone says it's a good live show or it's a good album, we know it wasn't because it was the producer's idea or the record label's marketing plan.'

The switch of musical emphasis toward country was a stylistic step away from the White Stripes' Detroit garage heritage. Similarly, the physical relocation to Memphis was indicative of their progression beyond the boundaries of the local scene. Despite this, Jack insisted the new location was something of a home-from-home. 'Memphis is kind of a natural place to go, because the South is so similar to Detroit . . . . Just the feel of it. People down there call Detroit a Southern city. And we went to New Orleans not too long after. It's a straight line down; Detroit, Memphis and New Orleans are all the same city. The way the roads look, the way the buildings look, the mood and the vibe of the city.'

Jack also identified Memphis's country and western heritage, and the avoidance of domestic distractions, as key factors. 'That's sort of a side note to it, this idea of being respectful to who's come before you, and probably done it better. But more important is just the confinement, for us to go to places where we're forced to work. We made a mistake with our second album, recording it in my living room. It's too distracting to be at home and do that kind of thing.'

The new album, by now entitled *White Blood Cells*, was slimmed down from a double to a single disc and would feature a mixture of old and new material. Maintaining his commitment to 'breaking things down', Jack announced that the record would contain 'no guitar solos, no slide guitar, no covers'. He also made use of some vintage material – 'Dead Leaves And The Dirty Ground', 'This Protector' and 'I Can Learn' all dating back to his days with 2 Star Tabernacle.

We change things around all the time. If we had a third person there, we'd have to have a structure and it would have to be rehearsed. *Jack White*

As Jack later declared, 'It was good to put them all together at once, put them all in the same box and see what happened.

'Sometimes there's songs that get put aside until it feels right to do them,' revealed Jack. 'The only thing that's consistent is that we don't want every song to sound the same, we never want each album to sound exactly like the last one. A lot of people say that, but it's just important to us. Not to be a two-chord garage rock band forever.'

Because much of the material included on *White Blood Cells* was familiar to the duo, the album was recorded at a cost of around $4,000 – and at breakneck speed.

'There were probably only three real days of recording,' revealed Jack. 'We really rushed the whole album, to get that feel to it, a real tense thing coming out of it. Then we got back, did one more day of recording and remixed it. By that time, the engineer was really on our side and everything. It came out a lot better. This is our first album we ever got mastered. It's really loud.'

Engineer Stuart Sikes had received a crash course in Jack's aesthetic sensibilities: 'Jack told me more than once not to make it sound too good. I knew what he was talking about – from recording at their house to a 24-track studio. We didn't come close to using all those tracks. Basically he wanted it as raw as possible, but better than if it was recorded in somebody's living room. He steered me that way, and I ran with it.'

However, in contrast to Jack's growing assurance in the studio, Sikes revealed that Meg was uncertain. 'Meg didn't really think they should be recording – she thought the songs were too new . . . . Meg is pretty quiet.

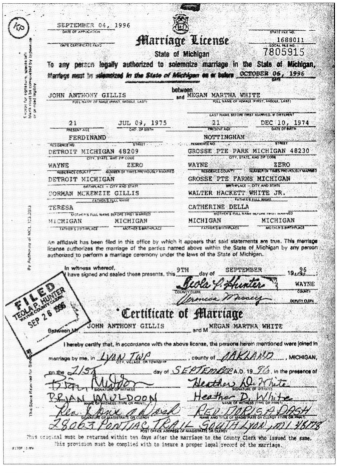

The simple truth that belies the game: John Gillis and Megan White's marriage certificate.

She sort of drank her bourbon and smoked a lot of cigarettes. I think Meg was a little nervous being in a big studio, bigger than what they were used to. The main thing I tried to do was make them comfortable so they could play well – with Meg, making sure her part didn't totally suck. She was pretty self-conscious about it.'

She need hardly have worried. In addition to providing the springboard that propelled the duo toward recognition, the sixteen-track *White Blood Cells* would be the White Stripes' most powerful and engaging album yet. From the moment the sibilant hiss of an amplifier announces the crashing opening chords of 'Dead Leaves And The Dirty Ground' to the final sustained notes of the elegiac 'This Protector', the patchwork promise of the band's first two albums is made whole.

Thematically, the record is a series of portraits of desperate romantic angst, viewed through a miasma of longing, regret and cynicism. It's this subtext, rather than any overt musical emphasis, that reflects Jack's country influences. That said, the country-punk hoedown of 'Hotel Yorba', and the use of simple acoustic string picking techniques on 'Now Mary' find the duo most assuredly in Tennessee.

Although at least half of the songs on the album find Jack howling into the swirling winds of sexual politics, familiar White Stripes' themes (innocence, simplicity, nostalgia) are also given a thorough work out. The third track, 'I'm Finding It Harder To Be A Gentleman Every Day', features the vocalist picking his way through the relationship minefield, under constant fire from notions of chivalry, sexism and prescribed gender roles. Buffeted by these conflicting dynamics, he pines for a simpler age, free from hazardous ambiguity.

I'm with Jack all the time, so it's kind of hard to say whether he's changed. Other people might have a better idea. Meg White

Likewise, a sense of longing for the certainty of childhood is represented by 'We're Going To Be Friends'. Reintroducing the young Jack's childhood sweetheart, Suzy Lee, the song demonstrates the duo's divine trinity of vocal, drum and guitar to achingly pretty effect. Jack's sweet vocals and simple acoustic plucking are underscored by Meg's simply stamped rhythm in the most beguiling of the White Stripes' nursery songs.

Similarly, 'The Union Forever' revisits and expands upon the revulsion from corporate greed of 'The Big Three Killed My Baby'. Comprised entirely of snippets of dialogue from Orson Welles' classic movie *Citizen Kane*, 'The Union Forever' highlights Jack's regard for both the film and its auteur director/star.

'There's a song in the movie, called "It Can't Be Love, Because There Is No True Love", that plays at this party they have in the Everglades . . . I was trying to play it on guitar, and I said a line from the movie while I was playing the chords. And it was like, "I wonder if I can rhyme that with something else from the movie?"' Irrespective of Jack's homage, copyright owners Warner Bros were apparently less than impressed and were reported to have considered filing a lawsuit.

Jack and Meg's relationship had dissolved less than a year earlier, and their subsequent divorce was to be finalised within weeks of *White Blood Cells'* recording. Jack's emphasis on matters of the heart imbues the album with a raw lyrical passion that compliments its wilfully unpolished production.

His vexation with the complexities of romance is dissected from a variety of perspectives. 'Fell In Love With A Girl' is a furious slice of over-revved garage that casts our hero at the sharp end of a romantic triangle. 'I Can't Wait's three-and-a-half minutes of boy/girl angst wouldn't have been out of place on The Go's debut album, while 'Expecting' exercises Jack's Robert Plant patented yowl to full effect, as he encounters the capricious demands of the kind of 'cold-hearted woah-man' that Led Zeppelin were fixated on. Singing of the lover's desperation to please his demanding sweetheart, 'Expecting' casts Toledo, Ohio in the role of romantic purgatory.

'People don't exactly go on vacation there. The girl in the song was sending me to do things for her, like run an errand to Toledo, which probably wouldn't be fun,' illuminated Jack.

The lyrics of 'The Same Boy You've Always Known' explore the dissolution of a relationship over time, and could be interpreted as auto-biographical. A less ambiguous piece of personal experience can be found in 'Little Room', a pointed drum and vocal blast that clocks in at under a minute. Reflecting on the song's lyrics, Jack observed, 'It's very interesting, none of the other Detroit bands were getting press and we didn't know

John Anthony White and Megan Martha White's divorce certificate.

why [the media] were picking us or why we were this lucky. We were still on the tiniest label in the country, we weren't exactly a huge success story at that point, so it was hilarious how prophetic that was.'

Both 'Offend In Every Way' and 'Little Room' indicate Jack's increasing dislike of pressure from the fans and the media. Of the latter Jack explained, 'It's about how . . . if you're a great painter and you're just painting in your room and all of a sudden someone sees it, then they're all, "This is great! You're genius! Let's have a show." So they have a show and everyone goes nuts. Then they're like, "OK, let's have another show," and now your inspiration isn't from where it used to be when no one knew about you.'

Jack's refusal to accept external influences is also evident in his dislike of encores. 'People get upset if they're asking for one and you don't come back. Or if someone asks you for an autograph and you don't give it to them. You say, "Come on, it's just kind of superficial." But people get really mad if you say no to things like that,' he sighed.

'Lately, we've just played one song at the encore. People were upset by that. Well, we don't have to do that. We don't have to come back at all.'

Aside from the feedback maelstrom of the instrumental 'Aluminium', the most radical new direction evident on *White Blood Cells* is the theatrical 'I Think I Smell A Rat'. Populated by baseball bat wielding punks straight out of *West Side Story* and punctuated by Meg creating the kind of clashing-cymbal sound described in the Old Testament, the song reflected the duo's love of Broadway musicals and show tunes in general. 'I like musicals a lot. Our parents played *Sound of Music* and *Music Man* and things like that,' revealed Jack.

Written the day before the band left for Memphis, 'I Think I Smell A Rat' made further use of Jack's earlier compositions. 'We had this song called "That's Where It's At" that we didn't put on the first album. [The lyric] was, "All you people know/Just where it's at now/walking down the street with a baseball bat now." It's about the kids in the neighbourhood. We weren't going to use that song anymore, and I played that chord, and "I smell a rat" popped out again. Meg played it with me and I started singing the lyrics from that other song about the kids in the neighbourhood . . .'

The country influences on *White Blood Cells* are further evident in its dedication to Loretta Lynn. Like many people, Jack's introduction to the country legend came via the film of her best selling biography, *Coal Miner's Daughter*. The movie, which earned Sissy Spacek an Oscar for the title role, recounts the singer's unlikely rise from teenage mother of four to the first female country artist to receive a gold album.

'I always kind of knew the name but it wasn't until I was a teenager and I heard a record somewhere and I just thought it was such a pretty voice so I watched the movie again,' recalled Jack. 'It's one of my favourite movies of all time and I just can't believe how great it was. I felt like I had always been missing something.'

Maybe it was Sissy Spacek or the big hair. I don't know. I thought she was really pretty and I still do. *Jack White*

Meg was also a big fan, having been similarly captivated by the film. 'Loretta spoke her mind, was so completely honest. She chose and wrote songs about things that mattered to women, that empowered them and made them feel more confident about living in a world where men's opinions always seem to matter more.'

In addition to the dedication, the White Stripes would pay further homage to Loretta by covering her song 'Rated X', which would later appear on the flip side of the 'Hotel Yorba' single. 'She has written so many songs, saying it like it is, and saying things that people didn't dare to say at the time she did it,' asserted Meg.

'In my opinion I just think she's the greatest female singer/songwriter of the twentieth century,' opined Jack. 'She's excellent. She's broke down so many barriers and did it just the right way. She's just so honest, which is exactly the most important thing about music to me.'

With *White Blood Cells* in the can, Jack and Meg headed out to road-test the new material on their first major headline tour. Following successful shows in Maryland and Massachusetts, their late February engagements in Hoboken, New Jersey and at New York's Bowery Ballroom would bring them under the scrutiny of the East Coast's hip cognoscenti.

Oh man, we don't want to be Led Zeppelin or Cream, or anything like that. *Jack White*

As one might expect, Jack had little interest in playing up to a terminally trendy crowd. 'We played Hoboken before we played New York,' recalled Jack. 'That was a horrible show. It felt like it was a crowd of critics. People had their arms folded, "OK, we're here, impress us." They weren't moving. After I was done, I just told the bar, "Man this crowd is terrible." And it was sold out. But it felt horrible. I don't play for that kind of crowd. That's not enjoying music or experiencing it. It's pure judgment, pure coolness, pure hipness.'

Fortunately, the full house at the Bowery Ballroom was far less self-conscious, responding to the duo with such zeal that Jack forgot himself and came back for a second encore. 'It's amazing that word of mouth got us so far,' he enthused. 'It just always feels like we're the flavour of the month.'

The next significant stop on the White Stripes' roadshow was the annual South By South West music festival, held each Spring in Austin, Texas. The festival is a huge independent music jamboree, started in 1997 and featuring over 200 bands. Sharing a bill with garage 'rock 'n' soul' combo the BellRays, the White Stripes treated a packed house to a storming show.

With the amps turned up way past eleven and Jack maniacally tearing chords from his Airline guitar, the duo created an enormous impression. In addition to selling out their stock of albums almost within minutes of finishing their SXSW set, Jack and Meg also grabbed the attention of *NME* journalist Stevie Chick. He quickly realised he was 'witnessing something special' and hurried back to Britain to sing the band's praises.

Following a brief return to Detroit, which included a triumphant sell-out show at the Magic Stick, the White Stripes resumed their cross-country trek. By mid-May the duo were in San Francisco, playing their most prestigious shows to date before a packed house at the Filmore. 'That was a pretty big deal for us,' bubbled Jack. 'They decorated the whole place with red-and-white decorations. It was just like, "Man, that's a really big way away from where we first started." To play a place that big and that historic.'

However, Jack was also conscious that playing larger venues ran contrary to his notions of simplicity. 'I went to a show – someone kind of big – and it was just too much. It was so not intimate – so overblown. I can't see us, with a two-piece band, getting to that point. I would think if we ever got such a big following it would just be so hard to do what we do. It wouldn't be intimate anymore it would just be a show. We'd like to keep it simple.'

Regardless of the guitarist's misgivings, the growing numbers of 'Candy Cane Children' were delighted to turn out for the band and regularly showed their appreciation in unique ways. 'People give us really nice presents,' revealed Jack. 'Somebody in San Francisco gave me a peppermint crash helmet. He does race cars and stuff. He gave me a crash helmet with peppermint stripes painted on it.'

'And that one girl with the jewellery, she made us silver pins, with peppermint,' added Meg, 'that was really nice.'

In a break with their previously established practice, Sympathy for the Record Industry opted not to issue a single ahead of the forthcoming album. With interest from the larger independent labels (including Sub Pop and the Beastie Boys' Grand Royal) in the air, the label cautiously put out a three-track sampler from the upcoming LP. Featuring 'Dead Leaves And The Dirty Ground', 'Fell In Love With A Girl' and 'Hotel Yorba', the seven-inch vinyl release became an instant collectors item.

We want to sound like we did when Meg first picked up the drumsticks and we discovered we could make it work. *Jack White*

Like the promo single, the sleeve and liner photography for *White Blood Cells* was by erstwhile Dirtbomb Pat Pantamo. Still adhering to the White Stripes' three-colour motif, the album's cover depicts Jack and Meg beset by half-a-dozen shadowy figures. The obverse is illustrated by a tableau straight from Walton's Mountain, showing the couple traversing a blood-red river that bisects a snow-white forest.

'The shadow-people might be bacteria coming at us, and Meg and I are the white blood cells. Or maybe it means white blood "sells" and the bacteria are media and music lovers . . . or maybe it means nothing at all,' offered a mischievous Jack. 'Perhaps on the back cover Meg and I are blood cells,' he continued, 'or perhaps she is on the dirty ground and I am in happiness . . . or perhaps I'm dragging her into a place she doesn't want to be or maybe she's pulling me out of it.'

Jack's liner notes are equally arch, but can be more clearly interpreted. Slipping into beat-poet mode, the guitarist announces the duo's readiness to *play*: 'Holding these truths to be judged forever – the mark, the string, the vibration all set and aiming to please. This sister with her hands, and this brother with his knees.'

Jack also alludes to the sense of separation from Detroit created by recording the album in Memphis: 'Our friends aren't here to help, but maybe that's the best help they could give.' In keeping with the double meaning suggested by the album's title, the biological theme of bacteria and blood cells is maintained throughout the liner art. 'The

White Blood Cells: *the duo's breakthrough album saw them beset, both literally and figuratively, by media 'bacteria'.*

name, *White Blood Cells* . . . is this idea of bacteria coming at us, or just foreign things coming at us, or media, or attention on the band,' explained Jack. 'It just seems to us that there are so many bands from the same time or before we started that were playing and are still playing that didn't get this kind of attention that we're getting. Is the attention good or bad? When you open the CD, it's a picture of us with these cameras.'

With the packaging finalised and no firm offer from any major label, Sympathy for the Record Industry pressed an initial 12,000 copies of *White Blood Cells* ahead of its 3 July release date.

Temporarily off the road due to a break in the band's touring schedule, Jack occupied his spare time by producing the Von Bondies' debut album, *Lack Of Communication*. The guitarist also made a rare solo appearance under his given name of

John Gillis, at the Golden Bowl bar in Detroit.

Perhaps surprisingly, the band hopped aboard the technological revolution, setting up an official website overseen by Ben Blackwell. As well as legions of online fans, the site attracted the attention of the makers of White Strips, a dental whitening product. 'I think the White Stripes website was too close to their website if you accidentally load it wrong. So they wanted to buy our website,' explained Jack.

To celebrate the release of *White Blood Cells*, the White Stripes announced three dates in Detroit. A launch party at the Gold Dollar would be followed by a show at Ferndale's Magic Bag the following evening, supported by Dan and Tracee Miller's Blanche, then a Saturday night gig at the Magic Stick with The Go in support. 'It was actually our booking agent's idea', revealed Jack. 'He called the places up. They thought it was a great idea. I thought they weren't gonna go for it, but they did. It seems like a pretty ballsy move for a local band to do that.'

Echoing Jack's fixation on the number three, the trio of shows were a sell-out success. However, the first gig was to be the last time the band played at the Gold Dollar. Owner Neil Yee stacked away the beer glasses for the final time on 18 August, before heading out in pursuit of his own rock dream as part of a band called Paper Tiger.

The critical response to *White Blood Cells* was overwhelmingly positive. Writing in *Rolling Stone*, Pat Blashill enthused, 'At a time when lots of folks would argue that rock is dead, a White Stripes ditty like the raging "I'm Finding It Harder to Be a Gentleman" actually sounds quite undead, like a love zombie or some other unstoppable monster.'

Similarly, the *New York Times* cast the duo as the perennial 'saviours of rock': 'With a stripped-down grace, the White Stripes . . . have achieved something uncanny: They have made rock rock again by returning to its origins as a simple, primitive sound full of unfettered zeal.'

All this attention is like an annoying fly. *Jack White*

Fittingly, the *Detroit Metro Times* was rooting for the home team. 'It didn't seem the White Stripes' infectious blend of pop, blues, punk and near-isolationist rumination could get any catchier. But they have. And it has,' observed Chris Handyside. '*White Blood Cells* is, simply, a storyteller-guitarist and a drummer battling disillusionment and optimism with simultaneously disciplined and raw-wound-exposed economy. The White Stripes are modernists in a post-modern world – they mean it, feel it and have worked hard to figure out how to express it.'

In *NME*, Victoria Segal caught the scent of a shift in the 2001 rock *zeitgeist*. 'As nu-metal bands proliferate at a rate that usually requires a visit from Rentokil, the unconverted could feel swamped by the tide of unhealthy mental filth rising up the charts. It's an unprecedented cosmic kindness, then, that for every band squawking at their parents like ungainly chicks demanding worms, America should be producing an equal volume of excellent guitar bands who haven't swapped their brains for a GameBoy Advance.' Focusing on the immediate appeal of *White Blood Cells*, she declared, 'Great songs, a great look and self-discipline, too. Rock 'n' roll might have been the ruin of many a poor boy, but the White Stripes are made guys.'

Irrespective of the band's individuality, it was necessary for the media to categorise the White Stripes, to pigeonhole them in order to sell them. With the nu-metal bandwagon running into the Linkin Park terminus, the press described any band with garage rock or proto-punk influences as a 'new rock revolution'.

It encompassed a pretty diverse selection of bands: the Strokes (a garage-influenced exercise in studied NY cool), the Hives (Swedish garage punks), Black Rebel Motorcycle Club (biker-chic rock *a la* Johnny Thunders), the Datsuns, the Vines, the D4.

When the success first came in England, and nationally, I think everyone around here was just like a little bit sceptical – like, 'Is this really happening?' *Dan Miller*

Essentially, any band evoking the appropriate elements of sixties or seventies rock could now reasonably expect a decent level of media coverage. Although many of these bands would later tour together, in the summer of 2001 all they stylistically had in common were their influences. In the same way as the music press trumpeted the re-discovery of early eighties indie rock two years later, any suggestion of a 'new garage scene' was wholly a media creation.

Like the White Stripes, most of these bands originated from within microcosmic local scenes similar to that found in Detroit. Despite the thriving garage underground in Sweden or New Zealand, there was no question of the kind of incestuous creative hot-housing that defined late 1980s Seattle, or London during the birth of punk. Still, despite being associated with a string of artists he had absolutely nothing to do with, Jack was keen to take advantage of the sudden interest. 'It worries us that it's not gonna last. I hope it lasts; I hope that we can do something with it.'

A fortnight after an impressive five-minute performance on CBS TV's *Late Late Show with Craig Kilbourn* (along with P. Diddy and Henry Kissinger), the White Stripes left for a tour of Britain. It would assuage any fears Jack might have had about enduring interest.

England was waiting for them – in addition to positive press in *NME,* they had caught the attention of the nation's most forward-looking DJ, John Peel. The veteran 61-year-old broadcaster's endless search for new and exciting music had led him to pick up *White Blood Cells* at a Dutch record store. 'It just looked so interesting, just the concept of it. I bought it, brought it home, listened to it, and started playing it on the radio,' recalled Peel. 'That sort of proper, over-the-top guitar playing – where you're actually playing something – has always been something I've enjoyed very much. So it was just

good to hear that kind of guitar sound again.'

Regular inclusion on John Peel's thrice-weekly radio programme ensured that import copies of the album were quickly snapped up in the UK. Indeed, so keen were staff at Rough Trade's Covent Garden branch that there were reports of them greeting prospective customers with the enquiry: 'White Stripes album?'!

A live session at the BBC's Maida Vale studios on 25 July captivated Peel to such an extent that he declared it one of the best performances he'd ever seen. Before the set, the DJ shared a meal with Jack and Meg and was duly impressed by their sense of musical history and perspective. 'British bands are so worried about being cool or being thought uncool, that they have to pretend that they're unaware of any music more than two years old . . . . I was amazed when Jack was perfectly happy to talk about things from my own childhood . . . when I saw Eddie Cochran and Gene Vincent play at the Liverpool Empire, four days before Eddie Cochran was killed in a car crash. When the White Stripes played that night, they ended their set with an Eddie Cochran song and a Gene Vincent song . . . . A British band couldn't do that – they don't have that kind of flexibility.'

I love that guy's voice. It sounds like he's just hit puberty. *David Lee Roth*

The following night saw the band's UK debut before a paying audience at the 100 Club on Oxford Street. Established primarily as a jazz venue, the club achieved near-legendary status after it hosted the UK's first punk festival in 1976. Since then, this tiny room, with its one-foot-high stage and intrusive pillars, has provided the setting for secret gigs by the Rolling Stones, as well as intimate shows by hip new bands. For those lucky enough to gain access to the White Stripes gig, escaping the densely-packed basement was not an option. A dripping-wet throng made flesh the hype with their heaving, sweating adoration. Performing in front of a backdrop comprised of the red City of Detroit flag, Jack and Meg thundered through a sinuous set described by one excited punter as 'the Carpenters suddenly possessed by the spirit of Led Zeppelin'.

Four days later, when the White Stripes returned to London following gigs in Brighton, Bristol and Oxford, Jack and Meg found the full force of the capital's music media laying in wait for them at Dingwalls in Camden. The sheer number of journalists and A&R reps present guaranteed that tickets for the show were at a premium, with touts outside refusing anything less than three times face value.

'You didn't stand a chance of getting a ticket,' complained MTV presenter Zane Lowe. 'Did I try? Oh, yeah, and I couldn't get one!' As Steve Jelbert wrote in *The Independent*, 'to describe the Detroit duo the White Stripes as "hotly tipped" is something of an understatement. Their first British tour has generated such excitement that label bosses hoping to snap them up have even paid for their own tickets. Music-busi-

Jack and Meg frame themselves for a photoshoot.

ness PRs have been seen in the mosh-pit, and, unbelievably, journalists have actually been spotted buying their records.'

Unfazed by frenzied expectations, the White Stripes put in another storming set guaranteed to keep interest at boiling point. Aware of the press's fascination with the ambiguity of their relationship, the duo playfully teased their would-be-inquisitors with a series of ever-more conspiratorial smiles and glances. As *The Independent*'s Simon Price observed, 'There's something distinctly unbrotherly about the way Jack turns towards Meg, leans into the microphone positioned near her drum kit and growls, "I wanna put her in a cave, and disconnect the phone . . ." There's a tangible sexual tension in the air, an incestuous latency.'

The divorcees fanned these speculative flames by ending their Dingwalls show with a cover of the Elvis Presley/Dean Martin standard 'Not The Marrying Kind'. In reference to the duo's coy manipulation of the press, Jack identified the ploy as a means of maintaining control. 'Because we'd heard that the English press would blow people up to "saviours of rock 'n' roll" level, then throw them away three months later, we thought this is what would happen to us. So we had to decide, are we going to let this destroy us or are we going to jump in head on and manipulate it so it works for us – and not let people push us around and destroy what we've been doing?'

The compelling Dingwalls performance drew universal praise. Steve Jelbert described the duo as 'The best live band on the planet,' while *The Guardian*'s Caroline Sullivan was impressed with the ferocity of the set: 'The nature of the music makes it easy to

I've not been affected by anything as much as this since punk, perhaps even since I first heard Jimi Hendrix. *John Peel*

crank up the amps, with no subtleties to be lost in the process, but you'd still swear you were hearing a whole platoon of nerdy twenty-somethings kicking around a blues-rock formula as old as the hills (but no less compelling for that). Even a cover of "Jolene", which argued that a middle-class Mid-westerner can croon as wrenchingly as the song's Tennessean author, sounded huge.'

As the band's brief tour drew toward its close, each enthusiastic review seemed to precipitate yet more media attention. Within a fortnight of their arrival in the UK, the duo had been featured in *The Guardian*, *The Times*, *The Sun* and the *Daily Mirror*. The music editors of the tabloids scrambled to outdo each other for superlatives. The *Mirror* pondered whether the Stripes were 'the greatest band since the Sex Pistols . . . or just a load of old hype' (helpfully, the paper arranged a premium-rate phone line to assist readers in deciding), whereas *The Sun*'s Dominic Mohan confessed to being 'blown away' amidst 'a devastating set of blistering guitar riffs performed at ear-bursting volume and breakneck speed'.

Perhaps most surprisingly, BBC Radio 4 covered the duo on their usually staid current affairs programme, *Today*. 'The *Today* programme covers music regularly,' explained the show's arts producer. 'Admittedly, it's probably not usually as loud or obscure as this, which is why I suppose it has been so remarked upon.'

Introducing the 'brother and sister duo', the broadcast identified the White Stripes as an antidote to the manufactured pop and pretentious miserablism currently infesting UK airwaves: 'Compared to Travis, Coldplay, Hearsay and countless other bands that dominate the charts, the White Stripes sound positively dangerous and rebellious.'

Following sell-out shows in Nottingham, Manchester, Leeds and Glasgow, as well as an appearance at the Witness festival in County Meath, Ireland, the duo rounded off their UK debut tour with a 'secret' gig at the Boston Arms in Tufnell Park, north London. Attended by such luminaries as Pulp's Jarvis Cocker and model Kate Moss, once again the press were out in droves. Andrew Male of *Mojo* was particularly impressed: 'They were sexy, they were frightening, they were sweaty, they were exciting and people were standing, mouths agape'.

In the *Daily Telegraph*, Andrew Perry expressed a sentiment that must have penetrated Jack's protective wall of suspicion: 'Where many bands become the "next big thing" by shouting louder than everyone else in interviews, Jack and Meg have achieved that dubious status solely on the strength of their music.' Two days later, the White Stripes' triumphant arrival on the UK music scene was cemented by their appearance on the cover of *NME*.

We were in Mojo, and we were really proud of that, because we really love that magazine. It meant a lot to us to be included with so many other great people there, even if it's just a mention. That made us kind of proud, because that's not bullshit, there's actually something backing it up. *Jack White*

Whereas most musicians would happily hand sell their grandmother in exchange for a cover feature in the UK's leading music weekly, Jack was less than delighted. 'We asked *NME* not to put us on the cover and they did anyway. We honestly thought the English press was going to chew us up and spit us out and we'd be left holding the bag.'

Wary of the media in general, and determined not to allow external influences to affect the White Stripes in any way, Jack believed the English press was inherently fickle. As he explained to *Today*, 'In America we heard that in England you can suddenly become big for a couple of months – then everybody forgets about you after that. We're trying not to take it too seriously.'

Having heralded the group as both the 're-birth' and 'future' of rock 'n' roll, *NME*'s support would confound Jack by showing no signs of letting up three years later. Irrespective of the storm of hyperbole the paper was kicking up, it was undeniable that a brief tour by a largely unknown outfit had created unprecedented levels of excitement.

'It was an extraordinary time,' recalled John Peel. 'The thing was, it wasn't hype. The *NME* has a kind of an obligation to find a new sensation every week, because that's what sells the paper. But I think people were just relieved at the simplicity and the directness of the White Stripes, and the fact they were making a noise they could identify with.'

Despite acknowledging that 'the music scene is divided and cut up into pieces, so there can be no single future,' *NME* journalist Stevie Chick remained unabashed: 'In a way, it's the *NME*'s job to blow things out of proportion. We've got to be out there discovering and championing new talent.'

Unlike in the US, the British music press has historically operated on weekly, as well as monthly, publishing schedules, which ensures that new acts are turned over at a faster clip than in the States. As *Q*'s Gareth Grundy exclaimed, 'all those pages: We need more fuel!'

However well-intentioned the *NME*'s effusive support might have been, Jack and Meg were singularly unprepared for the type of feeding frenzy the British press has become famous for. Simon Keller of Cargo (the White Stripes' UK distributor) explained the duo's bemusement: 'They're a bit punch drunk – nothing I've dealt with has been as meteoric as this,' adding, 'They don't really want to do any interviews, they're very cautious – they just don't want it to all get out of hand.'

The perception is that anything from Detroit is popular right now. There is a lot of excitement about it. It's good – the bands deserve the attention. *Meg White*

As Jack later explained to the *Detroit Free Press*, all the fuss meant little to him. 'It's kind of hard – we sort of feel like the flavour of the month, that there's nowhere to go but down. We're kind of hoping that all the fake attention we're getting lately will go away. In the meantime, we're trying to decide how to respond.'

The guitarist's tendency toward introspection led him to puzzle over the journalists' motivations. 'I know a lot of these writers and everyone have jobs to do. Maybe some people say it's the band they've been waiting for a while to write about; maybe some people are just doing their job because they were told to write about us. How can you tell? Reading one article to the next, you can't really tell what the scope of it is.'

Despite Jack's concerns, it seemed the hype was infectious: 'they could be as important as punk in triggering things off. There's so much processed music, just manufactured pap for the masses. It's an opiate for the disaffected youth whereas the White Stripes are a kick up the arse,' trumpeted Keller.

The success of the White Stripes' flying visit to the UK intensified record label interest in the duo. Despite overtures from Rough Trade supremo Geoff Travers (who had recently acquired the Strokes), on 24 September 2001 the duo signed with Richard Russell's XL Recordings for an advance reported to be in the region of £1,000,000.

Leo Silverman, XL's head of A&R, slipped smoothly into promo-speak: 'With their classic songs, their electric live performances and the raw, uncompromising nature of their music, the White Stripes are really doing something special.' The deal included giving *White Blood Cells* a full UK release by the end of the year and re-issuing the band's first two albums, previously available on import.

Meg, who had been cautiously hanging on to her waitress uniforms, remained quietly unimpressed with the peripheral trappings of success: 'we never really cared about all the things that other people cared about, you know? Like, people recognising me on the street never interested me. I've always been kind of suspicious of the world, anyway, so it's pretty easy for me to live in my own little world.'

Consistent with Jack's insistence that everything was secondary to the music, Meg asserted it was the aesthetic rewards that gave her the most pleasure: 'when somebody comes up to us and says they'd been discouraged with music and that we've made them feel a new energy for it. That's the nicest thing, that you've made people feel good about music again.'

Bands don't really get signed here, and a lot of bands don't have much hope for a lot of things, so the music's better. In L.A. or New York, bands have a Web site before they even play their first show. When you don't care about getting signed, you work on your music more. *Jack White*

Regardless of his distaste for the press furore around the band, Jack ended the tour by announcing his intention to return to the UK. 'Scenes don't mean anything to me. But we'd love to come back with the Detroit Cobras and the Von Bondies, and I'd be really glad if they did well over here. We'll try and get back while England likes Detroit for the next six months.'

The White Stripes returned to their home town, only to discover that the UK press had followed them across the Atlantic. Similarly, elite squadrons of A&R representatives were despatched to Michigan by labels fearful of missing out on 'the new Seattle'.

The comparison became ubiquitous – *Entertainment Weekly* pointed out similarities between Detroit and Seattle 'before grunge hit big', and, having caught the Von Bondies as the support act during the White Stripes' UK tour, *NME* was already preparing for blanket coverage.

'Seattle lasted for about two years on a buzz basis and five or six years commercially,' asserted *NME*'s Ben Knowles. 'I wouldn't be surprised if we put more Detroit bands on the cover by the end of the year. the White Stripes are probably the most exciting live band to come out of America in the last four or five years, but they're coming out of a city which seems to have many pots bubbling over, some really exciting musical talent.'

As Chrysalis Music representative Polly Comber had predicted during the White Stripes' UK tour, 'There could be a lot of money spent in the next few years on Detroit bands. People will certainly be going over there.'

Having spent many years operating within a city that was viewed nationally as a cultural wasteland, Dan Miller was tickled by the sudden interest. 'It was more comical than anything – nobody took it seriously . . . . I think there's still scepticism some people have about it. There's tons of people in Detroit who have no idea who the White

It's very hard to say, 'No, I'd rather not get famous from a cell-phone commercial.' *Jack White*

Stripes are – and I mean people who listen to music. It's pretty shocking. But in a way that's really good, because the White Stripes haven't gone out of their way to make themselves this real well-known commodity.'

Sam Valenti IV, head of influential Detroit dance label Ghostly International, believes the city's comparative isolation is integral to the unique nature of local acts. 'We're far away from the coasts, so people here just take their influences and sort of redefine them. Here the music is about being an outsider, hands down. It's definitely insider, cool-kid music, but it's not like New York and all self-aware, like "this is hip" and "this is trendy". It's about being from a place that's not the core and trying to make your own thing.'

The diverse nature of Detroit's parallel rock and R&B scenes serves to underline this. As *Spin* journalist Chuck Klosterman asserted, 'If you ask these bands if they play garage, most of them will tell you no. But there are certain things that hook all these bands together. It has less to do with sound and more to do with geography. The bands are already seeing what the perception of the White Stripes has done to their city, it's like a rock Mecca.'

Concisely summing up the parochial attitude, Ko Shih declared, 'Most of us don't listen to any music that's produced today aside from bands that we know in Detroit.'

Unsurprisingly, Jack too felt that there was no place like home. 'Unbiased, I've never seen bands write songs like they do here in Detroit. There's a couple different scenes in Detroit, and people say, "Oh that's just garage rock and they're rehashing sixties stuff," but a lot of these bands right now are just trying to write really good songs, and maybe people are missing the point.' But still, he claimed, 'It won't last. A year ago, [record labels] wouldn't even return a phone call.'

'Most of the musicians here are still dealing with shitty jobs, so it doesn't really feel like the record industry is paying any special attention to Detroit,' added Ben Blackwell. 'It's humorous, really,' chuckled Mick Collins, 'nothing's really changed. It's been happening for the last fifteen years. It's just that everybody's watching now.'

Further evidence of the growing interest came from outside the music industry, when clothing manufacturer Gap offered Jack and Meg an estimated (i.e. speculated) $100,000 to appear in an ad. The offer was indicative of Jack and Meg's growing status as hip icons. Gap's teacher-at-a-high-school-dance line of leisure wear, and nauseatingly saccharine adverts (gloriously lampooned by Rage Against The Machine in their 'Guerrilla Radio' video), had left the company in need of an infusion of cool.

But, favouring credibility over cash, the White Stripes chose not to take the loot. Ironically, as Jack soon discovered, turning down Gap hardly served to sidestep criticism. 'Gap wanted us to be in a commercial and we said "no" and everyone said, "why not?" It's almost as if, if people are willing to give you that much money, you are insulting everyone you know by turning it down. People's opinions about selling out seem to have changed over the years.'

From Jack's perspective, it was not a case of being opposed to commercial use of White Stripes material in any fundamental sense, simply that the nature of the ad didn't appeal to him. After all, the band had already played some shows sponsored by Levi's. 'If you handle things in a way where you're getting something out of it, like if our song was in some commercial that we thought was so just over-the-top, that it actually had some humour or something about it. For the most part, it just seems like a bad idea all the way around.'

Submitting to the whims of advertising directors seemed entirely contrary to Jack's determination to retain control. 'The thing with Gap was that they wanted us to appear in the ad,' he explained. 'So they would take us into the studio, they'd tell us what to wear, how to act and what to do. So that's them changing the perception people have of us; and that's what we don't like.'

The White Stripes' closest brush with national TV exposure thus far came on 10 October, when the duo were scheduled to appear on *The Late Show with David Letterman*. Despite being rehearsed, ready and in the 'green room', the programme overran and their performance was dropped at the last moment. Regardless of disappointed cries from the studio audience, and a provisional rescheduling for the end of the month, the last-minute cancellation marked the beginning of a long-running saga. 'They rebooked us being on that show nine different times. We always said, "yes," and then they'd come back and say, "oh no, U2 is going to play that night, sorry,"' recalled Jack.

Irrespective of the *Late Show* debacle, the public (or at least those with access to cable) only had a matter of weeks to wait before the White Stripes were beamed directly into their living rooms. Following the deal with XL, it had been decided to make 'Hotel Yorba' the band's first UK single. It necessitated making a video on the lowest of budgets, at the Detroit Hotel from which the song takes its name.

Unused to rock groups showing up to shoot footage, the hotel's management were initially reluctant. 'They wouldn't let us in,' revealed Jack. 'They thought we were from the IRS or something. It's a really seedy hotel, so I guess we just looked a little too respectable to get a room there. The funniest thing was we were sitting out in the van saying, "Man, we can't get in, I can't believe this," and just then NPR [National Public Radio] did a review of our new album, saying, "Here's the new song 'Hotel Yorba'." They started playing it, and we were just laughing.'

Shot by Dan Miller, the video simply shows Jack and Meg performing the song in one of the hotel's tiny rooms. It was quickly picked up by MTV2 and soon received regular broadcasts not only on both sides of the Atlantic, but also in Europe and Israel. All of which came as a surprise to Meg: 'When we made "Hotel Yorba" we didn't think that it would get played or anything like that.'

To promote the UK release of 'Hotel Yorba', a nine-date tour of England and Scotland was arranged, ahead of a series of dates in continental Europe. Before they left,

We really never were out to strike it big; success was never one of our main driving forces. Why else would we have recorded three albums with the smallest record label in the world? *Jack White*

the White Stripes played a triumphant hometown show at the Detroit Institute of Arts. Booked as part of the Institute's First Friday's programme, they were part of a cultural jamboree that included such delights as glass-blowing demonstrations and a Mexican paper-cutting workshop. After a low-key early evening performance (due in part to the deadening effect of the arts centre's marble walls), the duo returned to put on an exhilarating display for the packed second house. Performing in front of the City of Detroit flag, the White Stripes were hailed as local heroes. 'It was clear they were on their way,' recalled Greg Baise. 'I didn't go, but my *dad* did, and he thought it was just amazing.'

Heedless of Jack's worries about the ephemeral nature of their popularity in Britain, the White Stripes' mid-November return showed their popularity was still on an upward curve. The aftermath of Britpop, with its self-referential recycling of UK rock history, had brought with it a backlash that left British audiences looking to the USA for less contrived rock 'n' roll kicks.

Writing in the *Detroit Metro Times*, UK-based journalist Shireen Liane found that she had become hip-by-birth practically overnight. 'Americans haven't been so popular since World War II. Overpaid, oversexed, over here. I plan to be out of town the day that the backlash hits, but until then, life is *good*. If I had a pound coin for every time I'd heard, "Detroit is the new Seattle," during the past year, I'd be buying rounds all night, *plus* dinner and the cab ride home.'

A year before George W. Bush would do his darndest to change all that, the White Stripes blew back into the country on a tsunami of expectation. Two nights after a one-off show supporting Pulp at La Cigale in Paris, Jack and Meg kicked off their second British tour with a 11 November engagement in Brighton. Within moments of taking the stage it was clear that Britain had taken to the band with brio.

As the *Daily Telegraph*'s David Smyth observed, any suggestion that the White Stripes were a five-minute fad was spectacularly wide of the mark: 'Now that Jack and Meg White have returned to Britain for a sold-out tour, we have the chance to step back a bit and decide whether the hype was just heatstroke. By the seaside, on their opening night, the answer was a resolute "no". The White Stripes were extraordinary.' In the *Independent*, Simon Price (who was among the first to identify the band's qualities in the UK) permitted himself to gloat: 'I've said it once before, but it bears repeating: The White Stripes are the most vital band on the planet right now. Since the last time I said it, though, the rest of the planet has woken up to the fact.'

The day after the Brighton gig saw the UK release of 'Hotel Yorba', which was celebrated with an exclusive five-song set before an audience of 200 at Ocean in Hackney, east London. The performance was filmed by Channel 4 and recorded for broadcast on Jo Whiley's Radio One programme two days later.

You have to be on the road. You have to take what comes and kind of just go with it. *Meg White*

The flip side of the single featured a cover version of Loretta Lynn's 'Rated X', which featured vocal contributions from Meg. Both sides highlighted the well of country inspiration from which *White Blood Cells* was drawn. '"Hotel Yorba" is definitely Loretta,' revealed Jack, acknowledging the influence of the vocalist on the single's A-side, 'it's definitely a country song of ours. The cadence of it feels like Loretta to me. We recorded that album in Memphis and we ended up dedicating the album to Loretta.'

Jack's reverence for Loretta Lynn and her work is comparable to his regard for Son House, Robert Johnson or Blind Willie McTell. As he explains, 'On the way to Memphis we saw something that said "Loretta Dude Ranch" . . . There wasn't an ashtray in the car and Meg put her cigarette out through the window and I was like, "What? Don't throw your cigarette out in front of the house!" We ended up taking a tour of the whole place and we were just so alive. We were like two Japanese tourists.'

The following week saw more 'sold out' signs in Liverpool, Manchester, Glasgow, Edinburgh and Sheffield, while 'Hotel Yorba' began accumulating airtime and rave reviews. Nominating the song as Single of the Week, *NME*'s Alex Needham described the duo as 'Detroit's finest export since Motown and Madonna'. He also attempted to nail down the band's appeal. 'Consider the evidence: they make the world's most boring music (the blues) seem fresh and modern; they construct enormous walls of sound out of little more than a washboard; they make a thrift-store wardrobe of black, red and white look chic and, ahem, "directional"; and despite having no interest in – or, on the face of it, relevance to – the modern world, they somehow fit perfectly into 2001.'

The single sold healthily enough to provide the duo with their first Top 40 hit, peaking at number 26 in the UK chart and winning them their first *Top of the Pops* appearance. There was a huge demand for tickets – the tour's London finale at the Astoria sold out so quickly that a further show was arranged for the Kentish Town Forum on 6 December.

Albeit on a much larger scale, the Astoria was just as claustrophobic as the 100 Club had been four months earlier. 'I have never, in all my long life, seen the Astoria hosting such a vast collection of bodies as I did on this White Stripes night,' declared reviewer Michael Hubbard, writing for the Musicomh website. 'Wall-to-wall the bodies were, some still twitching with signs of life, pressed against each other, and gradually raising

'Hotel Yorba' – the first hit single.

the temperature of the place – despite the wind turbines blasting air out at either side of the stage. If that dreaded word "anticipated" could have any use, this gig was it.'

The Independent's Steve Jelbert enthused, 'How many bands leave you feeling mildly deflated after half an hour, on realising that the set's already half over? Newfound wealth or not, they're still the best live band on the planet. Who else could get a room pogoing to something out of a teach-yourself-guitar primer like the truly ancient folk blues "Boll Weevil Song"?'

As the White Stripes' first European tour wound its way through Holland, Germany, Italy, France, Spain and Belgium, interest in the band from the US label V2 materialised into a concrete offer. The American arm of über-hippie Richard Branson's sprawling Virgin empire, V2 provided a home to such diverse acts as pop-reggae legends Toots and the Maytals and balding technobore Moby. The White Stripes would be the label's first garage band, although Jack and Meg would shortly have the Datsuns for company.

We have a manager now, but all of the decisions have to come through us – which gets to be a lot of work. But it's better, because I like to be able to defend everything we do. *Jack White*

The deal itself was too good to turn down. In addition to an undisclosed higher royalty rate, the V2 deal ensured the White Stripes retained the rights to their recordings as well as the master tapes themselves. The contract also included a licensing arrangement for Jack to set up his own label, Third Man Records. Jack wasted little time in securing a contract for old Italy Records buddies Whirlwind Heat – whose debut album, *Do Rabbits Wonder?*, he subsequently produced.

V2's marketing and distribution was provided by the huge BMG conglomerate, far more sophisticated than anything a small label like Sympathy for the Record Industry could hope to match. The deal also included provision for a Stateside re-release of *White Blood Cells* early in 2002 that would see the album sell in excess of 700,000 units before the year was out.

The arrangement with V2 was signed in late November, as the band approached the end of their 22-date European tour. Acting as the band's legal counsel, Los Angeles-based lawyer Ian Montone revealed that, irrespective of V2's bountiful offer, the White Stripes maintained their customary scepticism toward big business. 'Initially, Jack and Meg didn't want to do any deal. But presented with this, they were interested. And they really liked [V2 president] Andy [Gershon]. He understands where the band wants to go and wants to let them develop that.'

It was almost certainly Gershon's insistence that he wanted to sign the band because he

liked their music, instead of for commercial reasons, that won the duo over. As Gershon explains, 'I asked one of the assistants here to make me a tape of . . . bands she thought V2 should be looking at . . . . She'd put on "Hello Operator". I thought it was absolutely magical, absolutely brilliant. I went out and got *De Stijl* five minutes later. Then I found the first record, and then *White Blood Cells* a day later . . . . When you look at it – the whole "brother-and-sister" thing, dressed in red and white, really raw – I figured this will never get on the radio. But I didn't care about getting hits.'

Back in Detroit, Ben Blackwell made no excuses and gave no reprimands for the White Stripes leaving Sympathy for V2. 'They never said they wouldn't sign a major label contract, and they walked away with the juiciest contract you could ever ask for. I mean, they got the masters in the end; Jack got his own label.'

No one set out to make a band to make it. Not having that attitude has probably paid off for people. *Jim Diamond*

Interest in any band in possession of a 313 area code continued to rise, with A&R men reportedly ringing record stores and local radio stations to ask who the hottest bands were. Sire Records supremo Seymour Stein (responsible for signing the Ramones, Talking Heads and Madonna) made several trips to the city, eventually securing the Von Bondies for parent company Warners. Likewise, the White Stripes' British label, XL, returned to pick up cabaret rockers the Electric Six, who had previously recorded on Flying Bomb Records as the Wildbunch. They would later create a mini-mystery as to whether or not Jack White appears as the mysterious John O'Leary on their 'Danger

(High Voltage)' single.

But, as Ko Shih observed, the intense focus on Detroit bands ensured that the intimacy of the local scene became a thing of the past: 'You used to be able to go to the shows and see the same 50 people there, and it was always the same 50 people. Now there are a *whole* bunch of people there, and a lot of the same 50 people you used to see aren't there anymore because they're out on tour.' However, another mainstay of the local scene, ex-Dirtbomb Pat Pantano, was keeping his feet firmly on the ground. 'What it boils down to is money,' he opined. 'No one's made any money yet.'

a box with something in it

5

Sometimes I want to give up, because I'm not what I wish I'd been – someone from the twenties and thirties, playing on a street corner, down South. *Jack White*

By the time the White Stripes had played the final show of their European tour, at the Kentish Town Forum, the duo had already begun recording new material for a fourth album. Speaking to *Kerrang!'s* Ian Winwood, Jack explained, 'We record albums very quickly. For example, everything's ready for the next album, we're ready to go with it. We write songs very quickly and we just want to get them recorded and done as quickly as possible.'

More than a month earlier, the group had booked into Toe Rag Studios in Hackney, east London, and recorded a whole slew of songs. The brainchild of production boffin Liam Watson, Toe Rag was fairly well-known for its strict use of vintage analogue recording equipment (the only exception being the necessary CD burner).

'It started when we found this sixties mixing desk,' explained Watson. 'Then we found an Abbey Road mixing desk – in 1982 EMI sold off all the Abbey Road equipment that they weren't using anymore, and a friend of ours had bought it but never used it. The Studer eight-track tape machine we bought off the BBC for £700, and it would have cost them £15,000 when they bought it.'

Fully kitted out for the mid-1960s, Watson completed the nostalgic ambience by decorating the space in greasy-spoon café chic, and donning the kind of white lab coat normally associated with eccentric British scientists.

With Liam Watson deriving his influences from many of the same sources as the White Stripes, Toe Rag quickly built a reputation for an earthy, 'organic' production sound. Before long, the studio had become established as the natural choice for a small cadre of retro-garage rockers. But the English garage rock scene of the 1990s was far less evident than its Detroit equivalent. The influence of sixties outfits such as the Count Five and the Sonics had failed to make any impact in Britain, and only attracted attention when early punk bands such as the Damned later cited them as an influence.

In some ways, the mid-seventies punk scene had been an amphetamine-fuelled adaptation of a reductive American garage sound that grew out of the rock 'n' roll roots of Gene Vincent and Eddie Cochran. Once punk had begun its protracted come-down, bands made up of punk refugees, such as the Television Personalities and the Milkshakes, traced the lineage and connected more directly with their original garage influences. Indeed, it was the Television Personalities (responsible for ironic punk classics 'Where's Bill Grundy Now?' and 'Part Time Punks') and Thee Headcoats (fronted by former Milkshake Billy Childish) who were among the first groups through Toe Rag's door.

Operating so far underground as to be (until recently) beneath the radar of the music press, Wild Billy Childish turned out vast quantities of garage-influenced vinyl throughout the eighties and nineties, as well as establishing a reputation as a gifted writer and artist.

Hailing from the thoroughly depressing southern hinterland of Medway in Kent, the former William Charlie Hamper had originally been a member of a short-lived punk combo the Pop Rivets. Following his tenure in the Milkshakes, Childish formed another minimalist garage band, Thee Mighty Caesars, who were later cited as an influence by Kurt Cobain. During the 1990s the guitarist and singer fronted Thee Headcoats, a group that spawned a more popular all-female spin-off, Thee Headcotees. As the decade drew to a close, Childish found himself at the core of a loose scene based around his vast creative output, regular Dirty Water Club gigs at the Boston Arms, and recording sessions at Toe Rag studios.

I did read somewhere that someone was relieved they were dating outside the family. *Holly Golightly*

Given that both the White Stripes and Billy Childish are singing from the same hymn book, it's unsurprising that, once introduced, all parties found much common ground. Childish, introduced to Jack and Meg by former Headcoatee Holly Golightly (who'd previously recorded on Sympathy for the Record Industry), in turn provided an introduction to Liam Watson and his musical time machine.

So, accompanied by Miss Golightly – who was to support the duo on their forthcoming London dates – Jack and Meg made their first visit to Toe Rag in November 2001. Speaking to *NME* the following January, an unnamed spokesman announced, 'They don't know what they're going to release from the sessions. The track with Holly Golightly [which later emerged as 'It's True That We Love One Another'] is basically a duet and they want to get a seven-inch out eventually, but we've no idea yet when or what the title is.'

Jack recalled how his duet with Holly came together. 'We were in town in London, and we were going to go check out Toe Rag and I called her and said, "Do you wanna go work on a song 'cause we're gonna check Toe Rag out, 'cause we've never been there before." And she's like, "Yeah." So I wrote that song for us to sing, in the hotel room, and finished it in about a half an hour . . . we went to Toe Rag and recorded it in a couple of takes.'

Touring commitments ensured that, even by their own intensive standards, the White Stripes' introduction to Toe Rag was brief. However, Jack found the studio entirely consistent with his ethos of self-limitation. 'It's so hard to find a studio nowadays that's devoid of that evil digital and computer technology . . . . To give you too much opportunity really destroys creativity. If you took an artist you respect and put them in a room with a broken guitar and a two-track recorder, something more interesting would come out of them than if you put them in some fancy L.A. studio with a million dollars to spend.' Meg nodded in tacit agreement.

The White Stripes and The Strokes was the beginning of more interesting people starting bands again. It's better than fucking Pop Idol. *Sir Elton John*

Meanwhile, while Jack and Meg were moving forward with some new material, their entire album catalogue was reissued by their new labels. In the face of rising demand, XL and V2 re-released *The White Stripes* and *De Stijl*, with V2 putting its distribution weight behind a second pressing of *White Blood Cells* for the American market.

Additionally, a second single was to be taken from *White Blood Cells* – the thrashy 'Fell In Love With A Girl'. Released in late February, it was accompanied by a video from French director Michael Gondry, depicting Jack and Meg as building-block style animations. The director, who had previously worked with the Foo Fighters, Bjork and Radiohead, keyed into Jack's obsession with De Stijl design movement for inspiration. 'As soon I heard the album, I loved the energy and kept playing ['Fell In Love With A Girl'] over and over. There's something charming and naïve about their use of black, red and white imagery. I made a parallel between that and the basicness of the colour of Lego blocks.'

'One day he came to a restaurant and he had Jack's head in Lego,' recalled a mildly disconcerted Meg. 'When someone brings a Lego sculpture of your head to dinner and says this is what the video's going to be, you pretty much say, "That's it, go ahead",' confirmed Jack.

'Fell In Love With A Girl' got to number 21 in the UK chart, and was later used by the BBC in in-house ads for their new digital radio service. Despite its moderate success, the healthy sales racked up by the reissues of the three previous albums meant neither XL nor V2 felt any urgent need to set a release date for a new LP. Touring remained the band's main priority. Major European and American tours were booked for the spring,

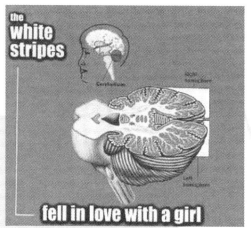

the
white
stripes

fell in love with a girl

The cover of 'Fell In Love With A Girl' provides evidence of Jack's fascination with surgery.

Jack and Meg's most exhaustive year of touring continuing with a series of dates in Australia and New Zealand. These shows, which included the Big Day Out Festival (an Australian equivalent of Lollapalooza), were swiftly followed by the briefest of visits home, before the band set off for England to promote 'Fell In Love With A Girl'.

During a brief lull in the tour schedule, Jack took the time to check out activity on the band's website. 'When I first put up the website and started sending out e-mails there were less than 100

When we play live, we're trying to close out all that's happened to the band over the last couple of years. *Jack White*

people getting them. Now there's like 21,000 some people on the e-mail list. It's so weird that in such a short period of time their fan base has grown like that,' exclaimed Ben Blackwell.

Seizing upon the site as a direct line to his audience, Jack posted regular messages about the band, the difficulty in finding a good chocolate malted, or anything else that he needed to get off his chest. In his initial posting, the guitarist described events surrounding the latest trip abroad:

'We are leaving for Europe to perform on *Top of the Pops* – the British Top 40 television show. I am kind of upset because we had planned to have Billy Childish on stage with us for the performance. He was going to be painting on an easel with his back to the camera, but the *Top of the Pops* people got a little confused and said we couldn't do that. Kind of funny that Kylie Minogue can have seven dancers on stage, and we can't have Billy Childish painting with us. Oh well, you can't always get what you want, you have to choose your battles.'

In the end, Jack appeared on the show with 'Billy Childish' written on his arm. Asked to explain the appeal of Wild Billy by a US radio station, Jack observed, 'He's really talented but he's quite popularly known as a bridge-burner. He doesn't have tolerance for a lot of things. That's the beauty of him though.'

The White Stripes hooked up again with the Kentish polymath when Childish's latest band, the excellent Buff Medways, supported the duo at the tiny 93ft East club in

Shoreditch. The low-key show was intended as a warm-up for the forthcoming European dates but attracted still yet further press attention. Also in attendance was what *Kerrang!'s* Joss Hutton described as 'every tittering fashion victim in London'. In her *NME* review of the gig, journalist Kitty Empire alluded to the band's non-stop schedule: 'If it's hard to imagine the White Stripes having a night off, it's impossible to conceive of them having an off night. Tonight's colour is pure red; tonight's sound is even more hot-blooded than ever before.'

Following the March dates in Holland, France and Germany, the White Stripes returned to the US for a short tour, the high point of which was a four-night residency at New York's Bowery Ballroom. Support was provided by a selection of acts including Whirlwind Heat, the Soledad Brothers, the Datsuns, ex-Cramp/Bad Seed Kid Congo Powers, and Detroit singer/songwriter Brendan Benson. In a posting on the band's official site, Jack singled out Benson for praise, declaring, 'this man is a master song craftsman.'

In the same bulletin, the guitarist indicated his frustration at being out of the studio: 'next month we are going to work on our next album which will be called *Elephant*. I'm tired of waiting around, I want to record. We have about twenty new songs ready to go, including a beautiful song sung by Miss Meg White.'

Following the tour's final show at Michigan State University, the duo barely had time to collect a pair of Detroit Music Awards (Outstanding National Album – *White Blood Cells* – and Outstanding National Single – 'Hotel Yorba') before heading back to Hackney to begin work on their fourth album.

With runaway sales of *White Blood Cells* showing little sign of abating, however, XL press officer Colleen Maloney told *NME*, 'They're just laying down the bare bones of tracks at the moment, just playing through them. They're really happy with it so far, but we're looking at the beginning of next year [as a release date].'

Jack was upbeat about the band's return to the analogue authenticity of Toe Rag studios. 'If we can't produce something that sounds good under those conditions, then it's not real to begin with. Getting involved with computers is getting involved with excess, especially when you start changing drumbeats to make them perfect or make the vocal melody completely in tune with some programme – it's so far away from honesty. How can you be proud of it if it's not even you doing it?'

The guitarist was delighted by the limitations imposed by Toe Rag's Spartan environment. 'It's very much like an English Beat studio from the sixties. Liam wears a white lab coat. It's not like an L.A. studio, where it's nicely carpeted and warm, with a cappuccino machine and video games between takes. It was freezing. I liked that, because it forced us to concentrate on what we were doing.'

'Nothing there was manufactured past 1965,' added Meg. 'The only things that are a little bit newer are the CD burners, but we hid them under the table, so basically we had the feeling we were somewhere completely different, in another time.'

Liam Watson's fundamental preoccupation with vintage fixtures and fittings ran parallel to the White Stripes' simple creative ethos. As with Jack's fixations with De Stijl and the number three, Watson's heroic tea-drinking and abstracted Englishness set him apart from the mainstream. Both producer and artist also shared a fierce commitment to producing music of few frills but genuine substance.

Having built the studio's dimensions with specific regard to the laws of acoustics, Watson's choice of an eight-track recording deck was based on technical considerations rather than any aesthetic whimsy. 'Pop music is listened to on two speakers at home,' explained Watson. 'So at the end of the day, that has to be finished onto a two-track format . . . . In 24-track, nothing is balanced as it goes down, it's all mixed later. The reason so many sixties records sound good is because the band would work on the song until they got it right, then they'd put it down.'

Having similar retrogressive ideas, Jack viewed the modern emphasis on hi-tech wizardry as little more than an expensive hindrance. 'Digital recording computers, Pro Tools and all that junk – I think that destroys the creativity of a lot of musicians. It's just too much and it distracts everything. Creativity gets buried under technology.'

Another of Liam Watson's productive eccentricities was the enforcement of a strict six-hour working day. Ensconced in a sympathetic environment with a suitably receptive producer, recording work on *Elephant* was completed in less than ten days at a cost of around £6,000. Although both expenditure and studio time were unbelievably low by anyone's standards, Jack maintained that such economy and brevity was simply a by-product of the duo's streamlined approach.

When did records start sounding a bit shitty? In the early seventies, when sixteen-track came in. *Liam Watson*

'When we are recording, we are like locked up in a box and exclude everything that could be disturbing. We decide in advance how long we want to spend in the studio and how much money we want to spend. When that's sorted, then we attack the pieces, the songs, and try to give each song its own personality and its own strength.'

Whereas fading nu-metal behemoths such as Korn and Limp Bizkit were spending millions of dollars, and taking months without end, just to create albums packed with self-indulgent whining, the White Stripes' disciplined method was a wake-up call to rock 'n' roll. 'I'm disgusted by artists or songwriters who pretend there are no rules,' affirmed Jack. 'There's nothing guiding them in their creativity. We could've spent six months making our last album. We could have recorded 600 tracks. Instead, we went and made the whole album, eighteen songs, in ten days.'

As with the previous three albums, the making of *Elephant* was underpinned by the White Stripes' adherence to the simple ideas that had served the band from the start.

'From day one, we purposely got involved in this box and with these limitations and chose not to grow and evolve,' Jack asserted. 'We still have the same ideas we had when we started. We break everything down to its most primitive state and involve the number three – storytelling, melody and rhythm; guitar, drums and vocals; red, white and black. Having these set parameters allows us to work best.'

Regardless of their stratospheric rise over the last eighteen months, Jack and Meg remained acutely aware of their strengths and weaknesses – steadfastly avoiding any additional embellishments or experimentation. 'I think we are ruled by simplicity and not complication,' mused Jack. 'We know our own limits fairly well, and we set our own limits and keep to it. We never did anything just to look cool or sound cool. Everything has to have a reason.'

With *Elephant* recorded and due for mixing in the autumn, the White Stripes took the opportunity to export a little of their hometown by agreeing to headline a 'Detroit Night In London', put together by *Q*. Performing at the Shepherds Bush Empire with long time cohorts the Dirtbombs and the Von Bondies, the duo attracted a stellar crowd that included members of the Breeders, Coldplay, Ash and Placebo.

We keep getting put with this bringing-back-the-blues kind of statement as a label for the band and I just wanted to break away from that because it's really hard to do that, being where we're from, even though that's the music that we really love and that I'm really inspired by. Most of the songs that had been sitting around were these piano-written songs that were more 'songwriting' type songs. I wanted to make a whole album of that. *Jack White*

With all three Detroit bands approaching top form on the night, the show garnered the by-now-customary rave reviews. *NME*'s Paul MacNamee described the group as 'the most visceral, arresting live band in the world right now', adding that, 'They may build their songs from chunks of the past, but they are our future.'

In *The Guardian*, music critic Alexis Petridis described the audience's near-hysterical enthusiasm: 'When they launch into "Hotel Yorba", the crowd erupts in a way that makes your average rock audience look like the model of genteel *politesse*. People lurch around with deranged abandon, beakers of beer are hurled in the air, a teenager clambers

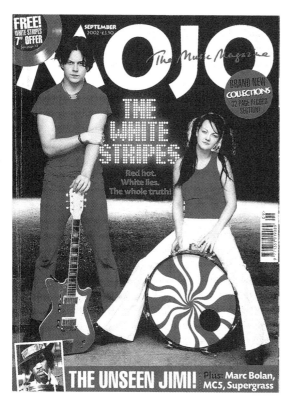

on the barriers before the stage and tussles with the bouncers. It is as if the White Stripes' reductive noise has unlocked an equally primeval state in their fans. The duo are as potent as rock gets in 2002.'

Having spent so many years toiling in the poverty of the Michigan underground, Dirtbombs drummer Pat Pantano found himself some-what taken aback: 'I'm sur-prised because I never thought it would happen in my life-time. There were always great bands in Detroit that nobody ever heard – it's about time.'

After a one-off Irish show at the 6,000-capacity Dublin Castle, which sold out in a matter of hours, the White Stripes returned to Detroit to hang out and play a series of high-profile shows at the Royal Oak Music Theatre, Clutch Cargo's and Chene Park. The full houses at these sell-out dates contained a sprinkling of veterans of the band's Gold Dollar days, many of whom were surprised at how far the duo had developed. As Detroit Cobras guitarist Maribel Restrepo said, 'at Royal Oak I saw a level of professionalism that had gotten really high. They had it down. I'm a cynical musician, but I couldn't quit watching. It's hard to entertain a whole theatre with two people. It was quite a feat.'

Dave Buick noticed the improvement in Meg's technique. 'She's gotten so much bet-ter as a drummer, but right from the get-go she was just perfect for that. She's gotten so much better, but she never needed to, really.'

Since Meg had become completely comfortable with her instrument, the White Stripes' collective confidence had grown rapidly. The engaging hesitancy often evident in the band's early performances was supplanted by an assurance that enabled them to dominate larger venues. 'At Chene Park, they owned that stage,' observed Greg Baise. 'There was a level of authority that Jack and Meg had on there. They knew exactly what they were doing.'

Although pleased to be back in Detroit, Meg found herself feeling slightly nostalgic for the 'old days': 'it still feels like home. Everyone you know is still there. We miss the little shows we used to perform. But it's fine. We still have fun playing at home.'

Following a performance alongside fellow Detroit native Eminem at the MTV awards show in Los Angeles, Jack and Meg played two dates at the local El Rey Theatre. They were swiftly followed by two sell-out nights at San Francisco's Filmore and a further run of North American gigs that took in Seattle, Vancouver and Toronto.

The rumours all stemmed from the fact that all of a sudden people paid us some attention and started to be curious about us. We didn't give a lot of interviews, so people didn't have a lot of information about us and they started to make up rumours. *Jack White*

Often arriving dressed in De Stijl-regulation red, black and white, the growing legions of Candy Cane Children at these shows bore testament to the band's spreading popularity. Jack was delighted to be reaching new audiences and aware of the potential for blues evangelism. 'When you're onstage at a sold-out venue, you kind of feel that . . . people don't know much about what's happening; they want to witness something . . . [or] people think they know everything about you, and they want to experience it in a different way. So the goal is to share with people, but you can sort of manipulate what they experience. If we can trick fifteen-year-old girls into singing the lyrics to a Son House song, we've really achieved something.'

However, for the White Stripes, the downside of the sold-out shows, rave reviews and media acclaim came in the form of the kind of media intrusion. 'When all of a sudden the whole media circus broke loose, we got really scared and were shocked,' recalled Jack. 'We didn't know how to handle it and what to say, so we decided not to give any interviews. Then we realized that no matter if we'd give interviews or not, the papers and magazines would still write about us because we were simply too popular and they wanted us in their magazines.'

As the band's profile grew, the manufactured controversy over their familial relationship refused to go away, fuelled by Jack's constant knowing references to his 'big sister'. Despite being the architect of all the speculation, even he reached the point where he found it wearisome. 'Frankly, we're kind of tired with all the attention on the brother-sister thing. The White Stripes are about the music, and we don't want that to be lost.'

The posting of Jack and Meg's marriage and divorce certificates on the *gloriousnoise* website kept the issue alive. However, while he may have been tired of fielding questions about it, Jack was still happy to lead unwary reporters astray, and refused to deviate from the brother/sister party line. 'The world is a gossipy place and people are always inter-ested in making up things. It is a problem that all bands have. If you have a male and a female member in a band people want there to be some sort of controversy when it is nothing of our doing really.'

In support of her pseudo-sibling, Meg perpetuated the conceit. 'I don't understand the attention on me, personally, as the drummer. I think that being out there playing the shows and recording and releasing an album should be enough. I understand the curiosity, I really do. It's just weird that [attention is] focused on me and my brother.' Perhaps sensing that his manipulation of the media was backfiring, Jack declared, 'We never wanted to be dissected by people. It became relevant to us that no matter what we said, nobody was believing it. It became a thing like we were sort of constructing lies all the time. And we were like, "if we wanted to do that, we would have come up with more interesting things to lie about."'

The posting of the certificates kicked off the inevitable controversy over their likely legitimacy. 'You just have to realise there is nothing you can do about that,' sighed Jack. 'The process is completely out of our hands. Someone showed me some press clippings they were saving for the band and they got a whole book of them in the last year. It was hundreds of pieces of articles and reviews and I swear only about two percent of it was actual interviews with the band.'

Elsewhere, another website revealed that Meg was not Jack's sister, nor his ex-wife – but an android. 'At the end of every night we have to plug her into the tour bus, plug her in and change her oil every three months to keep this band going,' confessed Jack.

Some of the craziness we just can't reveal to you because it's too crazy. *Jack White*

More whimsical evidence of White Stripes mania arrived in the form of a pair of homage/adaptations of their songs. First came *A Tribute To The White Stripes* by Diff'rent Stripes – a three-track single offering tinny synthesised reworkings of 'Hotel Yorba' and 'Fell In Love With A Girl', and a spectacularly dreadful reggae interpretation of 'I Think I Smell A Rat'. The single, which was put together by the same people who'd produced a similarly themed *Diff'rent Strokes* record earlier in the year, came in a cute sleeve depicting Jack and Meg as cake decorations.

Former Redd Kross bassist and Tenacious D session man Steve McDonald also post-ed his own downloadable versions of White Stripes songs on his website. Adding bass parts to tracks from *White Blood Cells* and pasting an image of himself onto the cover art, McDonald described his 'Redd Blood Cells' project as an affectionate tribute: 'It's not as if I wanted to take a shot at a band that dared make my instrument irrelevant. I really love their approach, so I just see this as taking being a fan to another dimension.'

Unperturbed by McDonald's heresy, Jack gave the venture his approval. 'I met him the other night . . . He told me about this and he said that he's adding, he's playing bass along with all of our songs . . . I think it's a great idea.'

The summer of 2002 saw the White Stripes hit the European festival circuit in earnest for the first time. Initially, it appeared the duo were struggling to adapt to playing on the immense stages. Despite being one of the biggest draws at the Main Stage, a slightly sub-dued set drew a lukewarm response from the usual herd of bourgeois Glastonbury hippies.

Uncomfortable with the vastness of such settings, Jack entertained serious doubts about the duo's ability to perform before big crowds. 'We don't have the potential to be like an arena act. I don't think a two-piece band really would come off in an arena-sized place. It doesn't really have any intimacy . . . . I like smaller clubs when people are more

The White Stripes at Glastonbury, June 2002.

forced to experience something. It is harder at a festival. I don't think electricity and day-light mix really well.'

Further outdoor shows in Denmark and Norway allowed Jack and Meg to find their festival feet. But, before they could get too comfortable, the White Stripes were whisked back to the US to play a series of four shows with the Strokes. Billed by the *NME* as a 'dream tour', the gigs saw the two bands sharing top billing, with the Strokes headlining for two nights in New York whilst the White Stripes took top billing on the opening Detroit leg of the tour.

Reviewing the Detroit show for the *NME*, Alex Needham paused to take stock of Jack and Meg's meteoric rise: 'The White Stripes have turned themselves into icons. And despite an intensive muckraking operation by journalists on both sides of the Atlantic, nothing can destroy their mystique.'

Rock 'n' roll is back, in whatever form. It's great to see a band like the Hives on TV – that wouldn't have happened five years ago. The joke in our mind was always, 'We'll take Detroit garage rock to the world'. We went to the mall a few months ago and they had 'garage rock' cut jeans on sale. *Jack White*

Previewing as-yet-unreleased tracks from *Elephant*, such as 'Ball And Biscuit', the duo overcame their discomfort with arenas to delight 6,000 enthusiastic punters who packed Detroit's Chene Park. Six nights later, at New York's historic Radio City Music Hall, the mini-tour of the year reached a fitting climax when Jack joined the Strokes on stage for an encore of 'New York City Cops'.

Afterwards, there was chaos on 51st Street, as huge crowds gathered outside the theatre hoping to catch a glimpse of the two bands. Strokes drummer Fab Moretti teased the throng by pretending to jump from one of Radio City's windows, while Jack bestowed his red T-shirt upon the multitude gathered below. Two weeks later, the same venue played host to the annual MTV Video Music Awards, where director Michel Gondry's 'Fell In Love With A Girl' promo came out on top in three categories: Breakthrough Video, Best Special Effects in a Video, and Best Editing in a Video.

Despite a well-received performance, the Whites were less than comfortable with the opulence of the occasion. 'It was good exposure but it was kind of scary to be in that forum and not being so sure about how you feel playing [to such a vast crowd],' admitted Meg. 'I mean, it was the difference between having a thousand people at a show and a million. For me it was one too many. We actually prefer never to play any place that would hold more than 5,000 people and even then that's tricky.'

Jack and Meg with their Breakthrough award at the 2002 MTV Video Awards.

The third single to be taken from White Blood Cells, 'Dead Leaves And The Dirty Ground'.

There was plenty of opportunity for further bonding between Stripe and Stroke, as the two bands were scheduled to appear on the same day's line-up at the twin Reading and Leeds festivals. Shoved out into the Friday afternoon sunshine at Reading, Jack and Meg drew an enormous crowd to the front of the Main Stage. Despite being bedevilled by sound problems early in the 45-minute set, the duo put in an outstanding performance in less-than-favourable circumstances.

Five hours later, Jack returned to the same stage to place the tin hat firmly on what *NME*'s Conor McNicholas later described as 'The greatest gig the Strokes have ever played on UK soil.' The intervening five hours between the White Stripes' and Strokes' sets had seen the traditional British festival weather take full effect. By the time the Strokes appeared for their headline set the site was like a medieval encampment, complete with bedraggled peasants, mud and pathetic attempts at starting fires that only added smoke to the icy gloom. All of which was instantly forgotten as the Strokes, whose rise to prominence had run directly parallel to that of the White Stripes, underlined their reputation with a mesmeric performance. As in New York, Jack joined the quintet on stage for the triumphant encore, the defining moment of that year's Reading event.

With the summer's festivals now over, Jack and Meg relocated to London to complete the remaining mixes for *Elephant*. It coincided with the UK release of the third single from *White Blood Cells* – 'Dead Leaves And The Dirty Ground'. Released on 2 September, the single also featured new versions of 'Suzy Lee' and 'Stop Breaking Down', originally recorded for BBC Radio One's *Evening Session*.

Less immediate in its appeal than either 'Hotel Yorba' or 'Fell In Love With A Girl', the new single stalled on the UK chart at number 25. Despite this, *Top of the Pops* executive producer and director Chris Cowey was so keen to have the band appear on the 2,000th edition of the show that the White Stripes were booked even though their single had dropped out of the Top 40.

Accompanied by an eerie Michel Gondry video (in which Jack is shown, lovelorn, amidst the ruins of a fictitious home he supposedly shared with a departed Meg – who herself appears as a ghostly superimposed image), 'Dead Leaves' was once again greeted by universally positive reviews: 'it's as fine a piece of noise we've heard this year. We have no choice but to salute its might and majesty,' wrote *NME*'s Imran Ahmed.

Further positive press came in the form of a cover feature in the September issue of *Mojo*. For once, the coverage delighted Jack. 'Meg and I are also extremely proud of the fact that our favourite magazine, *Mojo*, has put us on the cover. We are the first current American band to be on the cover of *Mojo*, and we couldn't be more happy, *Mojo* is an institution in our homes, you never throw an issue away, they're like encyclopaedias that you get once a month. God bless them for continuing to promote and discuss the finest artists that music has to offer, (not that we're one of them!)'

The week prior to the completion of *Elephant* found the White Stripes hanging out in London with various members of the Von Bondies and the Datsuns. After attending gigs by both bands in Camden, Jack and Meg ended the week by joining legendary ex-Yardbirds guitarist Jeff Beck on stage at the Royal Festival Hall as part of a retrospective celebration of his work.

When I come home from anywhere else I always have this sense of huge relief from all the craziness. You can't just wait for things to go away, because you just don't know if and when they ever will. Tomorrow it might stop, so I just try to make the best of the time. Meg White

With Meg's candy-swirl bass drum specially customised to incorporate the Yardbirds logo, the duo took the stage with Beck to perform seven songs. They were joined by Jack Lawrence, the bassist from Detroit outfit the Greenhornes, with whom Jack and Meg had spent some time rehearsing ahead of the show. Introducing himself and Meg to the RFH crowd with a nod and a wink toward their manipulation of the media, Jack announced, 'I'm Jack and this is my big sister Meg and we are the White Stripes. It's a great honour for us to be asked to fill the shoes of the Yardbirds.'

This show was to mark the duo's last British performance of the year. Within days the band had completed work on their long-delayed new album and returned to Detroit. In a posting on the White Stripes website, Jack announced the album was finally ready – although not for imminent release. 'We have finished the making, mixing, and mastering of *Elephant*, but won't let it out of its cage just yet, it needs to graze on the plains for a minute. Perhaps it's not what Meg and I think it is, perhaps it's the worst album we've ever made, or perhaps we'll all be surprised. We'll see I suppose, but at the time it was a good feeling, and it may come back and roost forever.'

Having brought mayhem to the streets of New York less than two months earlier, the

White Stripes repeated the trick on 1 October. A free midday concert in Manhattan's Union Square Park attracted a crowd of around 9,000, who reacted angrily when authorities cut the power to the stage, claiming the duo's set had ran over its allotted time. Despite frantic gestures from panicking officials, the band refused to leave the stage and Jack led the crowd in a singalong as Meg kept time.

'Thank you for skipping school and quitting your jobs to come here, it has made Meg very happy,' Jack told the crowd. The concert, for which the band had a mere 24 hours notice, was organised by Nissan, as part of a series of 'guerrilla gigs' sponsored by the car giant. Inevitably, the White Stripes' appearance at an event promoted by an automobile manufacturer drew some startled responses, and a little sniping to boot. Obviously, Jack's dislike of all things automotive was totally at odds with his taking the Nissan penny.

But then, the White Stripes, just an old-fashioned American gentleman and sweetheart at heart, were never likely to hit their audience over the head with an anti-capitalist manifesto. Both Jack and Meg have maintained a resolutely apolitical stance – refus-

Jack incites Union Square, October 2002.

ing to offer anything aside from the most innocuous response, when questioned on issues such as America's occupation of Iraq, for example. Lyrically and conversationally, Jack's focus is on personal, or sexual, politics.

Further criticism greeted the White Stripes' surprise appearance on *Saturday Night Live*. The show was hosted by Senator John McCain – a right-wing Republican and 'longtime admirer' of former US president Ronald Reagan, also known for taking self-righteous verbal pot shots at Eminem. Stepping in for R&B star Nelly, the Stripes provided the programme's closing musical number. They obviously engaged in no political badinage with the Senator. *NME* whipped up a minor shit-storm, however, by canvassing opinion from 'some viewers' who 'expressed surprise' over Jack and Meg's appearance on the same show as McCain. Oblivious to this non-drama, Jack seemed perfectly happy with the show. 'Meg and I want you to know that we are extremely proud of our performance. That is exactly how we want the White Stripes to be heard and seen, it was perfect.'

After a brief pause to complete production work on Whirlwind Heat's debut album, Jack rejoined his 'sister' to provide support for the Rolling Stones on two dates of their 40th anniversary *Forty Licks* tour. 'I can't believe that we've tricked people into letting this two-piece band get to this point,' enthused Jack.

It is weird to be sharing a cigarette with Nicole Kidman in the middle of Transylvania. *Jack White*

The shows took place at Toronto's Air Canada Centre and the Columbus Nationwide Arena. Having never caught the Stones live, Jack took the opportunity to do so and was suitably moved. 'They were still playing well. Watching them sound-check, they were all discussing how to play "Satisfaction". I was like, "They must have played this a million times, why are they even talking about it?" But they still care.'

Meg was equally starstuck. 'We chatted to all of them. Mick [Jagger] and Charlie [Watts] watched us from by the stage, and shook our hands when we came off. Charlie said he enjoyed it. That felt good. You can't ask for more than that as a drummer.' The White Stripes had broken through into rock's mainstream. Two weeks later, credit of a different kind was forthcoming from the *NME* – who named Jack as number one in the music paper's first ever 'Cool List'. Devised to 'celebrate the explosion of artists who've made music exciting again, who look good, sound incredible and live and breathe the essence of cool,' the 50 award winners also included Meg (at number six) and Jack's current girlfriend Marcie Bolen (at seven).

The White Stripes were finally compelled to take their non-stop show off the road when Jack was cast in a movie. He would play a Confederate deserter turned wandering folk singer in *Cold Mountain*, directed by Anthony Minghella. The film, based on a novel by Charles Frazier, is the story of a wounded soldier's journey from hospital to his wife and home in North Carolina.

Cast alongside Nicole Kidman, Jude Law, Natalie Portman and Renee Zellweger, Jack had been recommended for the part by soundtrack producer T-Bone Burnett – a critically-acclaimed performer steeped in American roots music, who had also played with or produced albums by Bob Dylan, Elvis Costello, Roy Orbison and Sam Phillips. Burnett had been impressed by *White Blood Cells*. Aware of Jack's love of folk music, Burnett suggested the guitarist to director Minghella, who was looking to introduce more music into the film. In addition to his bit part as the mandolin-picking Georgie, Jack also contributed five songs to the soundtrack album – including a new version of the Southern folk/blues standard 'Wayfaring Stranger'.

Regardless of his lack of prior acting experience, and the uncomfortable prospect of filming in Romania during the winter, Jack was thrilled to have been selected. 'I was flattered that T-Bone recommended me for the part. I was amazed that they picked me, and I felt really honoured and scared by it.'

'We cast him in *Cold Mountain* because of the songs,' explained Minghella. 'For his role he has to sing – that is why I got him. But then we discovered he can act too, so he sings and acts. It was beautiful, he really is a tremendous talent.'

Used to working quickly, Jack found the painstaking process of filmmaking heavy going. 'I was over there for a long time with pretty much nothing to do, but that's how it goes with movies I guess,' he observed. 'It was a lot of work. I don't think I could ever be a full-time actor – I don't know how those people do it.'

One sour note was sounded by alt-country singer Ryan Adams. Having spent much of the previous year covering White Stripes songs, and writing online hagiographies of the duo, Adams bitched, 'I was up for the part [in *Cold Mountain*] first and I turned it down. You know why? Because I didn't see acting anywhere on my job application to be a rock fucking star.'

Sensibly, Jack refused to be drawn into a war of words with Adams, who has stuck to his guns and is believed to remain interested in becoming a rock star.

Once location filming for *Cold Mountain* had been completed, Meg joined Jack at the wrap party for a special performance. 'It was surreal, very odd,' revealed Jack. 'There was this Romanian dance troupe there, and they had rehearsed a couple of numbers ['Fell In Love With A Girl' and 'I Think I Smell A Rat'] to dance with us when we played behind them. So there were these very clumsy Romanian dancers in these 1920s flapper outfits in this Communist cabaret theatre, with Nicole Kidman and Jude Law dancing in front of us. It was very odd.'

Once back in the United States, Jack headed to Tennessee to complete his work on the soundtrack album. This afforded him the opportunity to work with a number of venerable bluegrass musicians, such as Ralph Stanley. 'The whole thing was deeply humbling. I went down to Nashville to record the soundtrack and it was all the best bluegrass musicians, and I didn't even want to touch an instrument around those guys. I just said, "OK, I will sing, humbly sing." Much as I love American folk music, I didn't think that alone entitled me to be in that world.'

While Jack was in his customary blur of activity, Meg made the most of her time away from the tour bus. 'I was mostly being a hermit,' she admitted. 'Then I went on tour with some friends [the Soledad Brothers] for a little while.'

With the festive season approaching, V2 and XL issued a vinyl-only, limited-edition single, 'Merry Christmas From The White Stripes'. Essentially a reissue of 'Candy Cane Children', the most notable feature of the record is its B-side. Jack reads 'The Story of the Magi' while Meg sings an *a cappella* 'Silent Night' (before ex-hubby chips in to argue about the words). The track was described by *NME* scribe Pat Long as 'ace, mainly as an insight into their Christmas Day, pre-divorce.'

'We wanted to give a little gift to our fans,' expounded Jack. 'It was sort of in the tradition of the Beatles' Christmas greetings, the 45s from the sixties that they used to put out.' With a pressing of just 3,000 copies, the single became an instant collectors' item.

them chains, they're about to drag me down

6

It's so funny that when the aroma of money and fame is in the air, old friends will quickly step on your face to get to it. *Jack White*

As the early weeks of 2003 passed, expectation levels for the forthcoming release of *Elephant* started to resemble hysteria. With the album's official release date still around two months away, reviews appeared in the music press and on the Internet as promotional copies found their way into circulation.

In an attempt to limit the potential for piracy, the promo edition of *Elephant* was issued exclusively on vinyl, as a double LP. 'We didn't want any journalists who didn't own a record player writing about us,' joked Jack. Revealing that the album was 'dedicated to the death of the sweetheart,' he added, 'It's called *Elephant* to represent me and Meg's personalities in real life – majesty and regalness, and innocence and subtlety.'

As to how access was controlled to the promotional copies, Jack explained, 'We wanted to make the first listen more of an event. We wanted people to take part in it and that was a nice way to do it. It sort of became a nice artefact you can hold in your hands. I think we are approaching a dangerous age of invisible music with MP3s. I am going to be very sad if that actually happens where you don't hold a real album in your hand anymore.'

The fourteen tracks were issued on two records – 'it was a way to keep it stronger,' said the guitarist. 'Once you go past eighteen minutes on a side of vinyl you start to lose volume and bass. If someone goes to the trouble of buying vinyl we wanted them to get something nice. So we made it a double so the song quality was really good.' The following week, samples of the album art were distributed, depicting Jack in a C&W-style tasselled shirt and Meg in a simple white cotton dress, sporting a Loretta Lynn hairdo. 'We're "dying country stars" on the cover and that's one aspect of this whole death of a sweetheart idea. Modern country music has obliterated all honesty from country,' insisted Jack.

Given the relative ease of transferring vinyl into digital format, it was hardly surprising that, within days, it became possible to download tracks from *Elephant* from the Web. In an effort to limit potential damage, XL Records brought forward the date of

As their career starts to go stratospheric, Jack looks characteristically intense while Meg smiles passively at the camera.

the album's release to 31 March.

But John Peel, of all people, would incur the wrath of the White Stripes' label: 'I got the album a couple of months early, so I played a few tracks on it . . . some lawyers from New York with the record label let it be known that legal action would be taken if I continued to play tracks from the record . . . . Not to be able to play it really upset me.'

Meanwhile, the White Stripes previewed material from the forthcoming disc during a brief, unadvertised set at the Electric Cinema in London's Portobello Road. The performance was notable for Meg's live debut as a solo vocalist, singing 'In The Cold, Cold Night' from *Elephant*. 'I was really self-conscious at first about doing it, but I think I'm getting more used to being up at the front,' she later observed.

In a statement posted on the band's website, Jack displayed curmudgeonly disapproval at the way the album had been leaked. Sounding a little like Edgar Allan Poe, he scolded, 'I'm very sad at some of you for peeking at your Christmas presents before Christmas morning, can't you wait? I can. Well, I do. We want you to have it when we want you to have it, it's unfair that some get a taste and confuse others before they have the chance to have it for themselves, but the devil is at work here and you will pay for your impatience. This world of have it now, millisecond attention span and gross neglect for quality is getting old. I'm getting old too, watch me slowly die.'

When do I get a copy of the key to your world, Meg? *Jack White*

The artist's dismay at his audience was entirely apposite, given how concepts such as respect and patience lie at the core of *Elephant*. 'They want a backstage pass for every situation of the artist's life,' protested Jack. 'And they want to be able to say, "I heard the new album a couple of months before it was available in the shops." I don't like it at all because that is a way to manipulate the artist they claim to value . . . . It's like breaking into the studio of a painter and trying to get glimpses of a picture before he even finished it.'

Promotional copies of the album were reportedly sold online for anything up to £150. The first single taken from *Elephant* would be 'Seven Nation Army' ,due for release three weeks after the LP. Both single and album would be supported by a four-concert mini-tour of the UK ahead of gigs in the US. These were scheduled to begin in Wolverhampton on 7 April. However, these dates were put in immediate jeopardy when Meg slipped on an icy New York pavement, falling awkwardly and fracturing her left wrist in two places. 'It was during that time when we had a big snowstorm and everything was melting right after we got it, so everything was wet. And I was just walking out of a club one night and I slipped and fell.' Meg's arm was immediately set in a cast and, although a session for John Peel's radio show had to be cancelled, the wounded drummer was able to join Jack for a whistle-stop promotional tour of Australia.

Meg kept her cast 'pure', refusing to allow friends to sign it after her 2002 double fracture.

Described by John Peel as 'that necessary next step', *Elephant* was finally set before a salivating press and public. On this occasion the hype was entirely justified. As much as *White Blood Cells* had developed on the duo's first two albums, *Elephant* trumped its predecessor as a cohesive body of work. The album combines all the distinct elements found on the White Stripes' earlier output (blues, rock, garage, punk, country, folk and show tunes, the lyrical emphasis on childhood and relationships, Jack's axe virtuosity and Meg's primal beat keeping) to create a compelling *gestalt*.

'It's like you took all of our albums and sort of mixed them up. If you had to have one album that was a good example of everything that we do and sound like, this would be it,' attested Meg. But there's a definite sense of progression in how the songs about childhood now seem rooted in an earlier past, and the vexed question of male/female relationships now firmly to the fore.

'I wanted to get people to think about how they relate to one another – how the males and females relate, how the parents and sons and daughters relate, and bring up some ideas to see if they still mean something,' Jack revealed. 'What does the word "sweetheart" or "gentleman" mean nowadays? Has it changed in the last 50 years? Should we re-evaluate these words?'

Elephant opens with 'Seven Nation Army', a song that has its origins in Jack's childhood phraseology. 'I used to call the Salvation Army "Seven Nation Army" because I thought that's what the name was. So I was working around that and it just became a song about gossip.'

A sideswipe at intrusive journalists and nosy fans, the track begins with Jack's downtuned guitar being fed via an octave pedal to produce a sound very much like a bass. The use of the bottom end led to a slightly aghast Jack fielding questions about adding a bassist to the live show. 'That would break up the thing of vocals, guitar and drums. Somebody else there would bring this fourth component. If you're going to have four components, you might as well have twenty.' Another break with standard practice on 'Seven Nation Army' was Jack's double tracking of his vocal. 'It said in the *NME* I used a vocoder, which is a complete insult to me. I would never use such a horrible, evil tool.'

Elephant's initial thunderous charge is maintained by 'Black Math', a visceral slice of garage rock that Jack originally wrote for The Go. Like 'Seven Nation Army', the multi-tracked vocal on 'There's No Home For You Here' shows the White Stripes extending their self-imposed limits. The layered vocals produce a hysterical choir of Jacks, screaming opprobrium at a departing lover. Keen to emphasise they were not abandoning key aspects of their original remit, Jack explained, 'We still recorded it in one day, we still recorded it on an eight-track. We were restricting ourselves in that sense. But I don't know if it's something we could do live. I mean I love the idea that live and records are two separate things. I just don't know what I think about that song anymore. I mean, at the moment we did it and finished it, it was so explosive. It seemed like a gigantic explosion of a song.'

As a big brother to 'Dead Leaves And The Dirty Ground', 'There's No Home For You Here' is the White Stripes in full flight. An exceptional sonic rollercoaster of tortured axe gymnastics, the track takes the numerologically significant third spot in the album's running order.

'I Just Don't Know What To Do With Myself' is the only track on *Elephant* not to have been recorded at Toe Rag. Originally taped at the BBC's Maida Vale studios, this version of the 1960s Dusty Springfield hit is the finest re-working of a Burt Bacharach/Hal David number since the Stranglers casually sodomised 'Walk On By'. When questioned about his choice of a Bacharach cover, Jack enthused, 'I really love him. I love his songwriting. With this particular song, Meg was fond of it and wanted us to do it, and we started to do it live. I love it because I started recognising that it was really a blues song in its purest form, when you strip down the Bacharach production. The essence of the song was blues, so I really adapted to that.'

Musically, it's a song of two halves; beginning with Jack's subtle picking, it builds to a crescendo of howling guitar and wailing vocals. The sonic mayhem is held together by Miss Meg White's big bass drum in a way that underlines her importance to the White Stripes sound. The very simplicity of Meg's beat keeping, providing a grounding for Jack's guitar and vocal excesses, is a cornerstone of the band's uniqueness.

The shy, distinctly non-verbal stickswoman was also very much to the fore on 'In The Cold, Cold Night'. With the duo's cover of Loretta Lynn's 'Rated X' tucked away on the B-side of 'Hotel Yorba', 'Cold, Cold Night' was, for many, a first opportunity to hear Meg sing lead vocal.

The last record had no bass. This one has some bass. We're not against the bass. *Meg White*

'Jack wrote it for me to sing, so there'd be a way for me to sing on this album,' explained Meg. 'I told him I couldn't sing it, but he refused to believe me, so we tried it out.' A theatrical combination of moody organ and sultry vocal, this track too shows Jack testing the parameters that he himself dictated. Revealing how the song's unique keyboard sound was achieved, Jack explained, 'I'm on my hands and knees on the floor playing the bass pedals of a Hammond organ. If you listen closer – maybe on head-phones or something – you can hear the wood popping, like the pedals popping up and hitting the wood at times in the song. It sounds like someone knocking on a door or something.'

Following the piano and slide guitar sweetness of 'I Want To Be The Boy To Warm Your Mother's Heart', which sees the duo veering off into similar McCartney-esque ter-ritory as on 'I'm Bound To Pack It Up', comes 'You've Got To Have Her In Your Pocket'. A folky blues ballad reminiscent of acoustic Led Zeppelin, the track features no contribution from Meg and is possibly *Elephant*'s weakest moment.

'Ball And Biscuit' – named after the STC 4021 moving-coil omni-directional micro-phone, invented in the 1930s and still used by Liam Watson – finds the band evoking the noisier end of the Zep back catalogue and includes Jack cutting loose with a solo of

Page-like grandeur. 'It was a restriction I relaxed on this album,' confessed Jack. 'There's a few on there. I've always kept away from doing that, and I finally let myself do it for some reason. Sometimes, I would do it live. But since there's only me and Meg onstage, there was never much time to do that. It's hard to play rhythm and lead at the same time without losing people's interest.'

Lyrically highlighting the guitarist's numerological fixations, the song is peppered with references to the 'Third Man' and 'Seventh Son'. 'I think that one is going to be popular on the tour,' reflected Jack on 'Ball And Biscuit''s visceral appeal. 'I'm experimenting with that cocky asshole persona and that was an adventure for me.'

Like 'Seven Nation Army', 'The Hardest Button To Button' employs an octave pedal to give Jack's guitar a booming bottom end. The lyrical content has its origins in the writer's childhood. 'I thought that was a great metaphor for the odd man out in the family. It also comes from the sayings of my father, like, "My Uncle Harold has a ten button vest but he could only fasten eight."'

The UK cover of Elephant, *one of six different covers issued around the world.*

The remainder of *Elephant* sees the duo working through their diverse palette of influences. 'Little Acorns' is a fractured fusion of blues, garage, glam, punk and metal, 'Hypnotize' is a Sonics-inspired garage romp underpinned by Meg's relentless snare, and 'The Air Near My Fingers' features an electric piano reminiscent of the Small Faces.

The album's penultimate track, 'Girl, You Have No Faith In Medicine', is a kinetic rant about the capricious nature of women that again evokes Robert Plant's testosterone-fuelled angst. 'It's about the irritation I was constantly getting with females arguing about headache medicine,' offered Jack. 'Like, "Oh, I can't take Tylenol, it doesn't work." Whereas a guy would just take anything, he doesn't even think about it. It seemed like this tiny thing was a big, telling sign of feminine behaviour. In my eyes . . . . Not that one's better than the other, but they're different.'

I normally give Meg the headaches, not take them away. *Jack White*

'I don't know about that song,' added Meg. 'Makes me wanna smack him. A lot.' Her tongue-in-cheek irritation with her 'little brother' also surfaces on 'Well It's True That We Love One Another', a folky *ménage-a-trois* featuring Holly Golightly. 'Holly and I, we're in love, and . . . we were having a fight and Meg was breaking up the fight to get us all to be friends again,' explained Jack. In the lyric, that both parodies and capitalises on the band's personal mythos, Holly sings, 'I love Jack White like a little brother,' while Meg retorts with, 'I don't care because Jack really bugs me.' *Elephant* concludes with the cast and crew retiring to take tea. 'Liam Watson makes a good cup of tea,' smiled Jack.

The sleeve art of *Elephant* varied depending on where the album was bought, and in what format. 'I've separated the earth into three parts vertically,' Jack announced, enigmatically. 'There will be six covers, one for vinyl, and one for compact disc in each of the three sections of the globe. That way Meg and I know where you got it from, such as the vinyl in Australia will be the same as the vinyl in Japan, but different from the CD in South America, which will be the same as the CD in North America.'

Unsurprisingly, all versions of the sleeve art conformed to the usual colour scheme and were designed by Jack, assisted by former Headcoat Bruce Brand, with photography by Pat Pantano. Jack's liner notes testify to his distaste for the superficiality of modern society. 'We mourn the sweetheart's loss in a disgusting world of opportunistic lottery ticket holders caring about nothing that is long term, only the cheap thrill, the kick, the for-the-moment pleasure, the easy way out, the bragging rights and trophy holding.'

Having stuck his boot into the MTV generation, Jack later offered some clarification. 'It wasn't a political statement so much as a social idea about the attitude, you know – teenage girls with tattoos and body piercings, and the white boy from the suburbs who adopts a ghetto accent. There's this whole attitude that you have to be hard, like, right out of the gate. And the sweetness and gentlemanly ideas are really going away.'

'The message everywhere is it's OK not to care about anything. Everything can be judged, everything can be trashed,' added Meg. Despite the risk of alienating a chunk of the band's potential audience, Jack was delighted to report, 'People have said, "I totally agree, I just wish you wouldn't have said that." It's funny to shock people with normality. I mean, it's becoming an age of punk for the sake of punk, angst for the sake of angst. What are we rebelling against?'

As *Elephant* hit the shops, the steady trickle of pre-release reviews became a unanimously positive deluge. Leading the stampede was *Rolling Stone*'s David Fricke: 'Singer-guitarist Jack White and his ex-wife, drummer Meg – the undisputed king and queen of the new garage movement – finally romp and rattle like a fully armed band. It is a glorious thing to hear. It will be one of the best things you hear all year.'

Writing in the *NME,* John Mulvey pinpointed how the duo had progressed without any self-indulgent loss of focus: 'If the White Stripes hadn't become superstars, *Elephant* would probably sound pretty much like this. It stretches their musical parameters without betraying the tenets of rawness and immediacy. It sounds massive, but intimate.'

Mulvey's review was echoed by Jack's summation of the band's development. '*Elephant* is a good example that we were unaffected creatively. It felt like we were the same two people in the studio like we have always been. I think we have done a pretty good job of ignoring the unnecessary thoughts.'

Never listen to what other people say about you, because other people's opinions are usually tainted by emotions such as anger, jealousy or dissatisfaction with their own lives. I really don't mind criticism, just as long as it's constructive. *Jack White*

In the *Detroit Metro Times*, Chris Handyside spotted what was almost a paradox: 'Somehow, in making a record that feels so small and up-close, the Whites have managed to put their larger-than-life persona back into musical perspective.'

And so it continued. *Elephant* received overwhelmingly positive reviews in pretty much any publication that had its own rock critic. None of which impressed Meg unduly. 'I'm not really concerned about what the media thinks. I mean, we're really happy with it, so I think however well it does or doesn't do, it doesn't matter that much,' she asserted. 'It makes a bit of a difference when it's a fan who's saying something rather than a magazine. I like to hear what [they] think because [although] we make music for ourselves, we make it for our audience as well.'

Dan Miller certainly appreciated it: '*Elephant* is going off in another tangent, keeping in the spirit of things. It's about not being afraid to try new things, to not care if the garage devotees go, "What?! This should all be live."'

For Jack, the album's immense level of critical and public acclaim represented new possibilities. 'Now that people are paying attention, it's very interesting to me to show

how much you can actually do with just these three elements of vocal, guitar and drums. When we're writing songs and making records, it's very easy to just rock out or just play two or three chord things over and over again . . . It's harder to sit down and tell someone a story that they can relate to, that really makes sense to them.'

With a new album recorded and ready to promote, Ryan Adams performed a swift u-turn and leapt back aboard the White Stripes' bandwagon. In a posting on his own website Adams burbled, '[the White Stripes] record may be the best rock 'n' roll record ever made. No shit. I am so jealous of that guy. He is so tuned in, it's just incredible.'

'I wish he would quit trying to use us to get more press,' sighed Jack.

The relief after months of feverish anticipation, combined with the media's eulogising of *Elephant*, was enough to send the album straight to the top of the UK chart and to an unprecedented number six on the *Billboard* Top 200. While both XL and V2 were delighted by such healthy sales figures, Jack found himself drawn into conflict with Virgin when the company used the band's image without permission. Virgin had previously had discussions with the band about the promotion of their line of mobile phones. Despite the absence of any agreement, ads in both the TV and print media featuring images of the White Stripes were used to promote the product.

Given the large number of commercial endorsements the duo had turned down, it was hardly surprising when Jack went ballistic. 'You can imagine if Virgin cell phones had just come to us outright and asked if we'd do a commercial, we would have said, "No." But now they were getting a free commercial out of us because of this situation. [We asked Virgin], "When did we ever sign a fucking contract with you pigs?" and "When did we ever agree to point of purchase advertisements with our picture on it at stores?"'

Despite his annoyance, Jack had little time to dwell on the inequities of corporate capitalism. Only a week after the cast on Meg's injured wrist was removed, the duo played their first date in support of the album at Wolverhampton Civic Hall in England.

With the band scheduled to begin an American tour a mere three nights after their final UK gig, at Brixton, British fans were buoyed by the announcement that the duo would return to appear at the Reading and Leeds festivals. The White Stripes' first US dates since the previous autumn kicked off with two hometown shows at the Masonic Temple – the first taking place in the venue's smaller hall; the 1,000-capacity Scottish Rite Theatre – before moving on to New York. The 19 April concert at the Hammerstein Ballroom had sold out in seven minutes flat. It was particularly special for Jack and Meg as they were to be supported by Loretta Lynn.

'We just called her and said that we had dedicated our last album, *White Blood Cells*, to her and just wanted to say hello and see if there's a chance we could ever play a show together,' explained Jack. 'We ended up going and having dinner down in Nashville where she lives . . . She said, "I was sitting around the house and I was doing my hair and I heard the White Stripes come on, and it sounded like someone was breaking into a bank."'

During a well-received set that included accompaniment from Jack for 'Louisiana

Woman, Mississippi Man' and 'Fist City', the 69-year-old country legend told the crowd, 'This is a very special night for me, because I'm working with my idols, the White Stripes.' The show closed with Loretta joining Jack and Meg to perform 'Rated X', following a storming set which saw the guitarist dedicate 'Dead Leaves And The Dirty Ground' to Miss Lynn.

Delighted at this mutual admiration pact with one of his idols, Jack enthused, 'We really hit it off. There's some kind of connection with us. I feel really comfortable with her, and I think she feels really comfortable with me, which I'm really glad for because

Us women don't have a chance. 'Cause if you've been married, you can't have no fun at all. You're rated X. No matter what you do, they're gonna talk about you. I don't know what to do about it . . . Just let 'em talk, Meg. *Loretta Lynn*

I could see someone like me – the way I look or whatever – not being appealing or her thinking that maybe I wasn't down with the kind of music she does . . . She could tell that we had the same love for the same things about music.'

Reciprocating the affection, Loretta spoke of her amazement at the power of the White Stripes' live performance. 'When Jack and Meg walked out on the stage and picked up the guitar and sticks, well, it sounded like they had a big band up there. I just went into shock, I'm telling you! That Jack, he don't slow down for no one. When he hits that stage you can't control him. He's way *out there*, you know?' With their relationship cemented, plans were made for Jack to rejoin Loretta Lynn to produce tracks for her new album during the summer.

Back in the UK, the release of 'Seven Nation Army' saw the single enter the chart in late April where it remained for five weeks, peaking at number five. Issued as a three-track disc, it also featured covers of Brendan Benson's 'Good To Me' and the traditional folk standard 'Black Jack Davey'. The single was accompanied by an eye-catching video produced by Martin Fougerole and Alexandre Courtes – a French duo who had previously worked with their fellow countrymen, the easy-listening synth-botherers Air. The film was equally as abstract as Michel Gondry's Lego-inspired 'Fell In Love With A Girl', overlapping multiple images of Jack and Meg to produce an enjoyable, seizure-inducing stroboscopic experience.

The video, which skilfully manages to hide Meg's arm in a cast, was later nominated for Best Rock Video, Best Special Effects and Best Editing at the 2003 MTV Video Awards. *NME* installed 'Seven Nation Army' as its Single of the Week, leaving reviewer John Mulvey wishing: 'if only all rock star persecution complexes sounded as great as this.'

After a memorable four-night residency on US talk show *Late Night with Conan*

Jack fulfils his dream of playing with Loretta Lynn at the Hammerstein Ballroom, 2003.

O'Brien, during which the duo performed a different track from *Elephant* for each broadcast, Jack and Meg crossed the Atlantic to undertake their biggest European tour to date. Taking in Sweden, Norway, Denmark, Germany, Holland, France, Spain, Switzerland, Austria and Italy, the duo zigzagged across the continent selling out concert halls and delighting festival crowds.

The trek found the Whites in good spirits – an *NME* feature showed Jack, nattily attired in straw boater and red swimming trunks, indulging in backstage high jinks with Soledad Brothers Ben Swank and Johnny Walker at Bologna's Flippaut Rock Festival. Once the European dates had been completed the band would immediately return to the US for more dates.

'We don't usually do real long tours,' groaned Meg. 'We usually do like three weeks at a time. We just kinda need a break to keep up. You use up so much energy that you get exhausted quickly.' Although Meg may have found the relentless procession of shows hard work, constant gigging ensured nightly opportunities to gain confidence in her new role of vocalist.

Irrespective of the excited reception accorded Meg's singing debut on 'In The Cold, Cold Night', she was initially nervous about performing the song live. 'She doesn't like her own voice at all,' revealed Jack. 'I wrote that song for her to sing specifically. And she adapted to it, I guess. She likes it all right now, but she wouldn't tell you that.'

'It's becoming easier,' deadpanned Meg. As Jack later observed, Meg's natural bashfulness and quiet nature made her an unlikely solo vocalist. 'She's too shy. In songwriting and presenting something that you create to people, you kind of have to have an extroverted attitude and a little bit of ego or something, but not too much. You have to have enough that it makes you want to express yourself. It's almost a "look at me" kind of attitude. She just doesn't have that. She's very shy and she's super-polite and she won't speak unless spoken to.'

There's a lot of interest in bands like the Strokes and the White Stripes, it's a more pure, less marketed version. It's all part of this rock 'n' roll renaissance. We've got to find some heroes. *Zane Lowe, MTV*

However, Meg's reticence is underpinned by a firm sense of purpose. 'Meg's quiet, but Meg's power is in that she only speaks up when she has to,' confirms Ben Blackwell. 'She very rarely says anything, but when she says something it holds an awful lot of weight, and Jack always takes what she has to say into serious consideration.'

'Meg's a very cool chick', adds Maribel Restrepo of the Detroit Cobras. 'She's like all the Detroit rock girls – they party hard. Meg is a classic example that just because you don't play a lot doesn't mean you can't play. Meg has more swing than most drummers I know. It's hard to be put in the spotlight like that, but the first time they played *Saturday Night Live* and *David Letterman*, she was so at ease.'

Whereas the long road trip was improving Meg's confidence, Jack found he was becoming more patient with the demands of his growing public. 'I really don't like encores. I've learned to just be nicer about it. I used to think that stuff was lame, T-shirts were lame and encores were lame and autographs or whatever.'

With Pacific dates now scheduled for later in the year, the American leg of what was rapidly becoming a world tour saw the duo put in yet more storming performances,

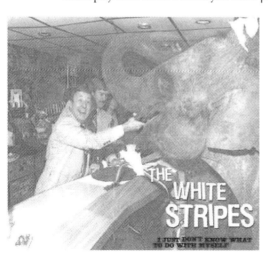

A real live elephant makes the sleeve of 'I Just Don't Know What To Do With Myself'.

including a show-stealing set at K-ROQ Radio's annual 'Weenie Roast'. The event, held at the Verizon Wireless Amphitheatre in Los Angles, saw the Stripes share a bill with Jane's Addiction, the Foo Fighters, Interpol and Blur.

However, on 9 July the band's touring schedule was abruptly curtailed when Jack was injured in a car crash. The accident, which occurred while Jack and his new girl-friend – actress Renee Zellweger – had been driving through Detroit, left the guitarist with a compound fracture of his left index finger. Miss Zellweger, whom Jack had met while filming *Cold Mountain*, escaped unhurt.

'This 75 to 80 year old woman drove right out in the

middle of the street, right in front of us. There was nothing I could do to get away from it. It was lucky that there was nobody seriously injured,' recounted Jack.

In addition to the injury, the incident provided the first public sighting of Jack and Renee together as a couple. Jack was customarily tight-lipped about their relationship, despite intense media interest that lumped the couple alongside Coldplay frontman Chris Martin and Gwyneth Paltrow – as evidence of a new trend for actresses acquiring 'indie' boyfriends. Certainly, dating a Hollywood star seemed a long way from the bucolic simplicity the guitarist was fixated on.

Initially it was hoped that the damage would only mean cancelling the most immi-nent gigs. In an interview with the *NME*, the guitarist recalled the moment when he realised the precise extent of the damage. 'I looked down and saw my finger was just destroyed. I immediately thought, "That's not going to be good, is it?" It was a multi-ple fracture – which means it didn't actually go through the skin but it shattered inside the finger. I can't write, I can't play piano, I can't play guitar, I can't do anything cre-ative. I can't even tie my shoes.'

Ever the numerologist, the fact that the accident occurred on his 28th birthday led Jack to believe he 'got off with a warning' – an idea based upon the notion that 27 is the 'year of rock 'n' roll death' (Jimi Hendrix, Kurt Cobain and Jim Morrison all died at that age).

Any hopes of a quick recovery were dashed when it became apparent that the fractures were not healing and surgery would be required. Three screws were duly inserted in the injured digit. More remarkably, the operation was filmed and made available on the White Stripes' website.

'The first thing that hit me was immediately people were saying, "Oh, you're cancelling all these shows in England," and people don't believe that this is really true. It needed something to show them that it wasn't just that we didn't feel like touring,' explained Jack.

The band were compelled to pull out of the remainder of the summer's festivals, with over twenty North American gigs re-scheduled to commence from mid-September. More positively, the taxidermy enthusiast with a collection of stuffed animals managed to gain a degree of pleasure from the footage of his operation. 'I've always been interested in those things. I always watch surgery documentaries on TV, and I just thought it was an inter-

I asked the doctor to film it if he could for me – 'cos I wanted to see the inside of my hand. *Jack White*

esting little film on its own because they were playing White Stripes music in the operating room. You see their face, then them opening the finger up, drilling screws in it, then the X-ray, and at the end he said it was beautiful. I just thought it was cool.'

Jack went so far as to view the filming of his operation as a graphic comment on press intrusion. 'People were confused about whether it was a step in the direction of letting people into our lives, which we don't usually do. But that was the statement: Letting you inside my body.'

Unable to play the guitar, Jack occupied himself by teaming up with Loretta Lynn in Nashville as production work got under way on the country legend's latest album, *Van Lear Rose*. 'Me and Loretta have become pretty good friends since last year, and I think we work together really well,' said Jack. The album was released in April 2004 to critical acclaim and healthy sales. 'I'm so proud of this, because it's the first album since her very first record where all the songs are written by her. It's Loretta like I've always wanted to hear her – Loretta like she should be heard. It really turned out perfect,' enthused Jack.

Elsewhere, some guitar segments that Jack had recorded earlier in the year appeared on New York DJ Mark Ronson's debut album, *Here Comes The Fuzz*. Ronson told *Rolling Stone*, 'There's a part at the beginning of the song when Jack is screaming in the guitar pick-up, "Here comes the fuzz! Here comes the fuzz!" I guess he was like, "Fuck it – that's the name of the song." It's cool. It sounds really dirty and Beastie Boys-ish.'

Meanwhile, Meg was determined not to miss out on the festival season entirely, and set off for Reading and Leeds in England. At Reading, the drummer joined Black Rebel Motorcycle Club guitarist Robert Turner to check out the Soledad Brothers' set and stayed for a blistering display by Wild Billy Childish's Buff Medways.

The second single to be taken from *Elephant*, 'I Just Don't Know What To Do With Myself', would spend four weeks in the UK Top 40, climbing to number six. As had become almost customary, it wasn't released as a single in the US.

If the sensational reworking of the old Bacharach and David number wasn't sufficient to cause raised eyebrows, the accompanying video certainly caused a stir. Featuring a bikini-clad Kate Moss making distinctly arthritic attempts to pole-dance, the promo, directed by Sofia Coppola, captivated the tabloid press in the manner that scantily-clad supermodels generally do.

Jack confessed to being less than cock-a-hoop. 'I wanted the dancer to be the ultimate

'The Hardest Button To Button' – the third of four singles to be taken from Elephant.

metaphor for someone that doesn't know what to do with themselves. And in the end I don't think that metaphor comes across. It becomes about selling sexuality . . . my first reaction was, "We've insulted Burt Bacharach. I hope he knows we weren't just trying to use an underwear ad to sell our album."'

Kate Moss is great to work with. I could watch her pole-dancing all day. *Sofia Coppola*

Thousands of left-handed mouse users disagreed, and the 'For European Transmission Only' clip was accessed more than 160,000 times during the first week it was available online. The single also included three additional tracks, a cover of Blanche's 'Who's To Say' and new versions of 'Lafayette Blues' and 'I'm Finding It Harder To Be A Gentleman', both originally recorded for BBC Radio. With any promotional gigs ruled out on account of Jack's injury, the duo filled in time by reuniting with long-time collaborator Michel Gondry to make the video for their next single, 'The Hardest Button To Button'. Further visual exposure came via cult film director Jim Jarmusch, who approached the duo to appear in his forthcoming short, *Coffee and Cigarettes*.

By September, doctors pronounced that Jack's injuries had healed sufficiently for the band to resume their live commitments. However, the insertion of pins into his hand caused unavoidable muscle trauma, leaving the guitarist struggling to stretch his fingers around the more demanding chord shapes .'I can't play C or D Minor, chords like that. I'm just going to have to do my best.'

But, despite his discomfort, Jack was overjoyed to find his enforced idleness at an end. 'It was a nice breath of fresh air for a second, but it was frustrating at the same time.' The White Stripes returned to live action on 13 September, before a sell-out crowd of 8,500 enthusiastic fans at the Greek Amphitheatre in Berkeley, California.

In a moving tribute to Johnny Cash, who had died the previous day, Jack recited the lyrics to the country genius's song 'I Got Stripes'. Supported by talented indie-rockers the Yeah Yeah Yeahs, the White Stripes fulfilled the dates they had missed during the summer, with Jack's commitment overcoming any limitations to his technique.

However, *Rolling Stone* journalist Robin Rothman was distinctly unimpressed by the duo's performance at the Denver Filmore. Pausing only to lech after Meg, Rothman moaned, 'The songs blurred like the years and spoken words slurred into one another, and the whole thing slowly turned into a bunch of electro pseudo-blues gobbledy gook . . . Meg's simplistic skin-pounding, her child-like delivery and coy posturing resemble a stunt more than they suggest unique technique or talent . . . . The only thing that made her a better choice than a drum machine was her partner's ability to control her tempo without physically pushing a button. Well, she's cute, too.'

Aware that such criticism, however facile, is the lot of the artist, Jack observed, 'I never thought that the White Stripes were this super original band. My argument is that

Meg steps to the mike for 'In The Cold, Cold Night' – Irvine, California, June 2003.

music is this long tradition of thousands of years. It's the same as if you tell some comedian a joke, he'll tell you that it's either pun or pathos or irony or satire or sarcasm . . . . And it's impossible to come up with a joke that's never been told. You've just got to come up with your way of telling it.'

Typically stoic, Meg was less concerned about critical brickbats than she was worried for the safety of her Candy Cane Children at the packed shows. 'I don't like people in the front row being squished you know. Most of the time the kids they rush in to get to the front and wait in the queue and everything, and they end up getting smacked on the head and being pushed forward all the time. It kinda distracts from the whole thing. I'm not into that, usually.'

With the backlog of gigs mostly cleared, the White Stripes departed for a gruelling tour of New Zealand, Australia, Japan and Brazil that would occupy the whole of October.

I think me and Johnny Cash would get along . . . Because I don't think we have anything in common. *Jack White*

While in New Zealand, the duo played a special show for a hall full of slightly bemused primary school children. 'Some of them were really into it. Some of them in the front row had their hands over their ears. It was kinda loud you know,' laughed Meg. 'But they seemed to be really into it. It's really cool because they had learnt a traditional Maori song that they sung back to us in the end. We did a few songs, "We're Going To Be Friends", "Apple Blossom", "Hotel Yorba" . . . We were just trying to do all the quieter songs.'

During the tour, the White Stripes were supported by antipodean garage band the Datsuns, who, along with the likes of Jet and the Vines, were leading the finest wave of groups to emerge from the Southern Hemisphere since Australian proto-punks the Saints. 'We were doing our best to support what was happening down under from the get go. We bought the Datsuns out on tour with us and we have played shows with the D4,' confirmed Jack.

By the time the tour hit Japan on 21 October, both Jack and Meg were beginning to tire from the constant demands of gigging and promotion. 'That's kinda hard work really. It just tires you a lot, 'coz you are busy all day. You get no time to really relax. But we needed to do them [interviews] 'cos we haven't got a chance to do as much press here as in the States,' yawned Meg.

During an interview with *Q*, reporter John Harris noted the black rings around Jack's eyes and that 'for the first twenty minutes of our encounter, whether from exhaustion or nerves or some other complaint, his hands gently shake.'

If the White Stripes needed a rest, it wasn't going to happen immediately on their return to the USA. After an appearance at the New Orleans City Park Voodoo Festival, the duo had just a week to draw breath before setting off on yet another North American continental tour.

Starting at the Eagles Ballroom in Milwaukee, Jack and Meg would play seventeen dates in twenty days, taking in three Canadian gigs, a three-night stand at New York's Roseland Ballroom, and two more homecoming shows at the Masonic Temple. In a complete break with tradition, the tour's final show, at Cleveland's Agora Theatre, saw the duo joined on stage by a bassist – Whirlwind Heat's Steve Damstra. The addition of an extra pair of hands for 'The Big Three Killed My Baby' allowed Jack to indulge in a solo of monumental proportions.

Irrespective of such experimentation, Jack was quick to reiterate the band's manifesto. 'A lot of people want to second guess when we'll get a bass player . . . We like living in our little box. Not changing and not evolving.' Added Meg, 'I've never played with a bass player before, so I wouldn't even know. It wouldn't feel like it's missing, I just think it's normal . . . I prefer it that way so I only have to concentrate on Jack.'

Honest to God, girls never come up and talk to me and I've never worked out why. I think it's because I'm not very cocky and girls always like cocky guys. *Jack White*

Backed by a cover version of the Soledad Brothers' 'St. Ides Of March', 'The Hardest Button To Button' was issued as a single on 17 November. Supported by the Michel Gondry video, which had been filmed in New York during Jack's lay-off, the disc crashed into the UK chart at number six.

An immediate staple of MTV's scheduling, Gondry's film attracted considerable attention and praise, even without the aid of a supermodel or a pole. As with 'Fell In Love With A Girl' and 'Dead Leaves And The Dirty Ground', which he also directed, the Frenchman came up with a simple but effective idea completely distinct from the band's earlier promos. Using a stop-frame technique, Jack and Meg are transported through the streets of New York and its subway network while an ever-changing array of equipment appears and recedes around them.

Filmed over three gruelling sixteen-hour days and utilising 32 identical drum kits and amplifiers, as well as sixteen mike stands, the video also features a walk-on appearance from the maverick multi-instrumentalist Beck – a long-time friend and admirer of the band. The shoot was labour-intensive.

'We didn't hire any lights, so we had to do it all with natural light,' explained the director. 'I had it very carefully planned out, though I realised Jack was doing different expressions for each take and I didn't correct him. I initially told him to watch it, but I realised the result would be very electric because each frame would jump around with different expressions.' 'We trust Michel,' added Meg, 'and he has come up with so many great ideas.'

On 13 December, Jack and Meg attended a launch party at the Magic Stick to mark the release of Blanche's new album, *If We Can't Trust The Doctors . . .* During a support

Jack and Meg face the cameras at the 2004 Grammy Awards.

set from Brendan Benson, Jack reportedly became involved in a fracas with Von Bondies front man Jason Stollsteimer, who was at the show with his wife and bandmates Marcie Bolen and Carrie Smith. According to Stollsteimer's management team, Jack spat in the face of their client and 'punched him in the head repeatedly'.

Depending on whose version of events one chooses to believe, the Von Bondie subsequently threw himself, fell, or was knocked to the floor as onlookers restrained Jack. Once the dust had settled, Stollsteimer's representatives swung into immediate action, wasting no time in posing their man for a photograph that showed him sporting a black eye with a small amount of blood spotted around his face. A statement was immediately issued accusing Jack of an 'attack . . . without warning or provocation'.

Describing the immediate fallout from the confrontation, Detroit journalist Ryan Suit commented, 'The few who witnessed the fight stood around in shock, while others began wondering if it really had been Jack White and Jason Stollsteimer tussling on the floor in front of them.' According to Suit, 'Throughout the entire incident and aftermath, Meg White sat calmly on a speaker at the far edge of the stage.'

Shortly after, Jack, who had suffered several cuts to his injured left hand, released a statement of his own through V2: 'Jack White was involved in a bar room altercation over the weekend in Detroit. Jack White defended himself as any normal person would have under the circumstances.'

With Stollsteimer's legal team pursuing the matter, a week of discussion with the Detroit police ensued before Jack was charged with aggravated assault on 22 December. Speaking at a press conference, Wayne County Prosecutor Mike Duggan asserted that no exceptions would be made for anyone who committed an assault, especially the famous. 'It seems that far too often celebrities think that the law doesn't apply to them. So many don't understand the impact they have as role models on young people. This just can't be tolerated.'

Speaking on his behalf, attorney Wally Pisczatowski retorted, 'Jack obviously knows he's not above the law. He's been a positive spokesperson for the city of Detroit, not only locally but across the US and abroad as well. He's helped a lot of people in this community and that should not be forgotten.' On 14 January 2004, Jack attended a hearing at Detroit's 36th District Court. The guitarist entered a plea of 'not guilty' and Judge Donna Robinson Milhouse set the trial date for 9 March, releasing White on a $5,000 dollar bond with no restrictions being imposed on his travel.

The dispute between White and Stollsteimer had been simmering for some time. It had its roots in events following the release of the Von Bondies' debut album, *Lack Of Communication*. Like many other Detroit bands (the Soledad Brothers, the Dirtbombs, Whirlwind Heat and Blanche), the Von Bondies had benefited from Jack's endorsement of their material, and were exposed to new audiences by being invited to tour with the White Stripes.

When *Lack Of Communication* was released, Stollsteimer and his band were more than happy to accept the publicity accorded the album on the strength of Jack's involvement. However, Stollsteimer seemed to grow weary of questions about his benefactor, and began criticising Jack's production work for failing to capture the Von Bondies' 'true sound'. Obviously, such comments were guaranteed to excite the media.

But, as Dan Miller later observed, 'If you go around saying shit about Jack after Jack produced your record for free, let you practice at his house for free, paid your air fare to go on tour with them . . . and then you start slagging them in the press. That's the real damage to Detroit. He's done that with other people as well.'

Although many observers noted how the break-up of Jack's two-year relationship with Von Bondies bassist Marcie Bolen hardly served to improve relations, it was the criticism of his production technique that Jack found particularly hurtful. In an interview published some three months before the brawl, *NME* journalist John Mulvey asked Jack whether the White Stripes' success had caused any resentment within the Detroit rock community.

'Everyone's been a really good family,' he replied, 'except for the Von Bondies. I don't know what their problem is. They've really lost their minds, it's ridiculous. The singer has really gone off the deep end. He's very mean spirited.'

I still live in the same house I was born in. But I had my chair reupholstered by someone else; I don't do it myself anymore. *Jack White*

Indeed, Stollsteimer's negative publicity-seeking had caused him to be ostracized from the local scene. 'It's too bad Jason got hurt,' sympathised Dan Miller, 'but in a way he was like a dead man walking. The guy had been very weaselly and said a lot of shit about a lot of people. It could have been 50 different people who ended up doing what Jack did.'

'He's been that way for a while,' confirmed Jack. 'I produced that band, got them a record deal. Detroit is such a great family and they're kind of a sore thumb. I don't speak to them. When you get burned consistently, there's no point in forgiveness any more.'

Although neither party has publicly disclosed the spark that kicked things off, it's worth noting that Stollsteimer had a new album to promote. His constant references to the new product's superior production must have antagonised the creatively sensitive Jack.

Ironically, following the release of *Pawn Shoppe Heart*, interviews with the Von Bondies largely concentrated on their connections with the White Stripes. Speaking to *Kerrang!* in January, who observed 'little evidence' of any enduring injury, Stollsteimer claimed he'd been continually 'misquoted' in his criticisms of Jack's production work. However, rather than supporting Stollsteimer's claims, his comments in *Pawn Shoppe Heart*'s press release served merely to strengthen the accusations levelled at him by local bands: 'We were never happy with our first record. It's always been a challenge to capture the power of our live show but I think we've come a lot closer this time.'

While the Von Bondies were in the UK to tour behind the new record, Stollsteimer wasted little time in stirring the pot some more. 'I'd get sick with anger if I saw [Jack White] again,' he whined.

It's debatable whether the Von Bondies really needed to promote themselves through constant references to the White Stripes. Although patchy, *Lack Of Communication* is by no means a bad album. The band's main strength lies in Don Blum's powerhouse drumming, which is to the fore on the album's excellent title track (which also features Stollsteimer doing his very best impersonation of Jack's vocal style).

Similarly, *Pawn Shoppe Heart* had received positive reviews despite veering in a more polished commercial direction, which saw the band move to a pre-teen audience with an appearance on children's pop show *CD:UK*. The band also achieved a UK Top 40 placing with the first single to be taken from the new LP, the catchy 'C'mon C'mon'. A recent tour in support of Funeral For A Friend further elevated the quartet's British profile, although attendees at Northumbria University greeted Stollsteimer with cries of 'There's Only One Jack White'.

Once the 9 March trial date rolled around, lawyer Wally Piszczatowski spent much

Jack looks on anxiously as his attorney makes a point at Detroit's 36th District Court, March 2004.

of the day locked in negotiations with prosecutors. With Jack reluctant to prolong proceedings, it was decided he should enter a plea of guilty to assault and battery. A deal was struck whereby the original charge of aggravated assault was dropped due to Jack's guilty plea to the lesser offence.

Passing sentence, Judge Paula G. Humphries ordered Jack to pay a total of $750 in fines and damages. Additionally, he would be compelled to attend anger management classes and was prohibited from initiating any further contact with Stollsteimer.

'We're happy that the most highly celebrated bar scuffle in the history of Detroit has finally come to an end,' Piszczatowski wryly observed. Rather than answer questions from the journalistic throng, Jack issued the following statement: 'I regret allowing myself to be provoked to the point of getting into a fist fight, but I was raised to believe that honour and integrity mean something and that these principles are worth defending. And that's how I live my life.'

Despite the bad taste left by the impending court case, a triumphant year for the White Stripes ended in good spirits with a New Year's Eve show at Chicago's Aragon Ballroom. Joined by the Flaming Lips, who filled in for the band at the T In The Park festival while Jack was nursing his injured hand, the two groups performed a version of 'We're Going To Be Friends' just before the clock struck midnight.

'It's two minutes before the countdown,' Lips vocalist Wayne Coyne informed the 4,500 revellers. 'So get out of the bathroom and find who you want to be with.' Coyne then smeared Jack with some of his trademark fake blood before the entire ensemble launched into a ballsy re-working of 'Seven Nation Army'. Before ending the show with the White Stripes' traditional finale of 'Boll Weevil', Jack announced, 'This is the last song of the night – Walk home hand in hand and hug your mothers and fathers when you get there.'

Further festive cheer came in the shape of applause from the media. In addition to three Grammy nominations (including Album of the Year for *Elephant*), the White Stripes dominated the music press's end-of-year polls. Both *Mojo* and *Q* acclaimed the album as Best of the Year, while it ran in second in *Kerrang!* and *NME*. With both Jack and Meg remaining well-placed in the music paper's second annual Cool List, the *NME* readership added to the duo's groaning sideboard by making 'Seven Nation Army' the winner of the Best Single category.

The early weeks of 2004 saw the band return to the UK to perform a short series of sold-out shows, including two nights at London's cavernous 14,000-capacity Alexandra Palace. These concerts were the biggest the band had undertaken, reinforcing their hard-won stature amongst rock's elite. While both Jack and Meg are notoriously uncomfortable with playing for such huge crowds, their popularity is such that arena-sized gigs are likely to become the norm. Similarly, the constant glare of publicity is something the band are gradually becoming accustomed to.

'Our goals have always been really low,' insists Jack. 'Success to us has always been not having to listen to anybody, and doing whatever we want to do, and not having to have a day job. Everything else was gravy on top of it, you know? We haven't really been

Jack and Meg thrill the crowd at a free concert in Union Square, New York, 2002.

forced to do things we don't like to do very much at all.'

With work on a new album scheduled for the latter part of 2004, and a mountain of touring commitments that include some of the festival dates the duo missed during 2003, it seems that Jack has simply too much on his plate to be overly concerned about his image in the press.

'It is sort of best to just put it away and think about it later. I will enjoy it later in life. There is too much to think about right now to be concerned with what people think with what we are doing. Something is happening and it is electric and I want to feel that the vibration that is happening right now when I am onstage or recording. That is what I want to focus on.'

However, despite his strict code of ethics, Jack confesses to enjoying at least one aspect of the White Stripes' success. 'When I go out to eat now, I get anything I want. I used to look at the specials or look at the menu, and now I just think about what I want to eat and just ask for it.'

Gastronomic delights aside, Jack foresees a day when the White Stripes will reach the end of their highly individualistic road and has recently suggested the duo will split after 'one or two more albums'.

As he explains it, 'When we're just not relevant to ourselves anymore, and it feels like we're being repetitive and doing it just for the money. If we cross some line where we just look at each other onstage and it's worthless, because we're so far away from where we started, then we're just going to have to stop. I refuse to beat a dead horse or do it just for the money. I couldn't live like that.'

Whatever the band's lifespan, the White Stripes will leave an important body of work as their legacy, and, as far as Jack is concerned, that's all that matters. 'In twenty years time all that people will remember is the music.'

discography

Singles

Let's Shake Hands/Look Me Over
Closely
(Italy Records IR-003) **1998 – USA**

Lafayette Blues/Sugar Never Tasted So
Good
(Italy Records IR-006) **1998 – USA**

The Big Three Killed My Baby/Red
Bowling Ball Ruth
(Sympathy For The Record Industry
SFTRI 578) **1998 – USA**

Hello Operator/Jolene
(Sympathy For The Record Industry
SFTRI 619) **2000 – USA**

Lord Send Me An Angel/You're Pretty
Good Looking (Trendy American
Remix)
(Sympathy For The Record Industry
SFTRI 645) **2000 – USA**

Handsprings
(Double A-sided single with the
Dirtbombs' 'Cedar Point '76', given away
with *Multiball* magazine – Extra Ball
Records XTR 005) **2000 – USA**

Party Of Special Things To Do/China
Pig/Ashtray Heart
(Subpop Singles Club SP527) **2000 – USA**

Dead Leaves And The Dirty
Ground/Fell In Love With A
Girl/Hotel Yorba
(Sympathy For The Record Industry
Promo SFTRI 662P) **2001 – USA**

Hotel Yorba/Rated X
(XL Recordings XLS 139) **2001 – UK**

Fell In Love With A Girl/I Just Don't
Know What To Do With Myself
(XL Recordings XLS 142) **2002 – UK**

Fell In Love With A Girl/Let's Shake
Hands/Lafayette Blues
(XL Recordings XLS 142cd) **2002 – UK**

Fell In Love With A Girl/Love Sick/I
Just Don't Know What To Do With
Myself
(XL Recordings XLS 142cd2) **2002 –
UK**

Jolene/Handsprings/Hotel Yorba
(Live)/Love Sick (Live)
(V2 Promo V2DJ-27739-2) **2002 – USA**

Dead Leaves And The Dirty
Ground/Stop Breaking Down (Radio
One *Evening Session*)
(XL Recordings XLS 148) **2002 – UK**

Dead Leaves And The Dirty
Ground/Suzy Lee (Radio One Evening

Session)/Stop Breaking Down (Radio
One *Evening Session*)
(XL Recordings XLS 148cd) **2002 – UK**

Dead Leaves And The Dirty Ground
(V2 1-track promo V2DJ-27750-2) **2002
– USA**

We're Going To Be Friends
(V2 1-track promo V2DJ-27772-2) **2002
– USA**

Red Death At 6:14
(3,000 given away free with *Mojo* magazine, XLS MOJO) **September 2002**

**Merry Christmas From The White
Stripes**
(*Candy Cane Children/The Reading Of
The Story Of The Magi/The Singing Of
Silent Night*)
(V2 63881-27769-7, XL Recordings
WSXMAS 1) **2002 – UK**

**Seven Nation Army/
Good To Me**
(XL Recordings XLS 162) **2003 – UK**

**Seven Nation Army/Good To
Me/Black Jack Davey**
(XL Recordings XLS 162cd) **2003 – UK**

**Seven Nation Army/In The Cold, Cold
Night**
(XL Recordings Promo XLS 162dj) **2003
– UK**

**I Just Don't Know What To Do With
Myself/Who's To Say**
(XL Recordings XLS 166) **2003 – UK**

**I Just Don't Know What To Do With
Myself/Who's To Say/I'm Finding It
Harder To Be A Gentleman (Peel
Session)**
(XL Recordings XLS 166cd) **2003 – UK**

**The Hardest Button To Button/St.
Ides Of March**
(XL Recordings XLS 173) **2003 – UK**

**There's No Home For You Here/I
Fought Piranhas/Let's Build A Home
(Live)**
(XL Recordings XLS 181) **2004 – UK**

Albums

The White Stripes
1999 USA
(Sympathy For The Record Industry
SFTRI 577)
2001 UK
(XL Recordings XLLP 149)

Seventeen tracks: *Jimmy The Explorer/ Stop Breaking Down/ The Big Three Killed My Baby/ Suzy Lee/ Sugar Never Tasted So Good/ Wasting My Time/ Cannon/ Astro/ Broken Bricks/ When I Hear My Name/ Do/ Screwdriver/ One More Cup Of Coffee/ Little People/ Slicker Drips/ St. James Infirmary Blues/ I Fought Piranhas*

De Stijl
2000 USA
(Sympathy For The Record Industry
SFTRI 609)
2001 UK
(XL Recordings XLLP 150)

Thirteen tracks: *You're Pretty Good Looking For A Girl/ Hello Operator/ Little Bird/ Apple Blossom/ I'm Bound To Pack It Up/ Death Letter/ Sister, Do You Know My Name?/ Truth Doesn't Make A Noise/ A Boy's Best Friend/ Let's Build A Home/ Jumble, Jumble/ Why Can't You Be Nicer To Me/ Your Southern Can Is Mine*

White Blood Cells
2001 USA
(Sympathy For The Record Industry
SFTRI 660)
2001 UK
(XL Recordings XLLP 151)

Sixteen tracks: *Dead Leaves And The Dirty Ground/ Hotel Yorba/ I'm Finding It Harder To Be A Gentleman/ Fell In Love With A Girl/ Expecting/ Little Room/ The Union Forever/ The Same Boy You've Always Known/ We're Going To Be Friends/ Offend In Every Way/ I Think I Smell A Rat/ Aluminium/ I Can't Wait/ Now Mary/ I Can Learn/ This Protector*

Elephant
2003 USA
(V2 VCP164165)
2003 UK
(XL Recordings XLLP 162)

Fourteen tracks: *Seven Nation Army/ Black Math/ There's No Home For You Here/ I Just Don't Know What To Do With Myself/ In The Cold, Cold Night/ I Want To Be The Boy To Warm Your Mother's Heart/ You've Got Her In Your Pocket/ Ball And Biscuit/ The Hardest Button To Button/ Little Acorns/ Hypnotize/ The Air Near My Fingers/ Girl You Have No Faith In Medicine/ Well It's True That We Love One Another*

Acknowledgements

The following sources have proven invaluable in the researching of this book; Periodicals; *Kerrang!, Rolling Stone, NME, Bang!, Q, Mojo, The Guardian/Observer, The Daily/Sunday Telegraph, The Times/Sunday Times, The Independent, The Daily Mirror.* Websites; *gloriousnoise.com, nme.com, bbc.co.uk, grunnenrocks.nl, whitestripes.com, white.stripes.com, whitestripes.host.sk, metacritic.com, dotmusic.com, drownedinsound.com, efestivals.com, playlouder.com, xfm.co.uk, thego.info, questia.com, flyingbomb.com, musicremedy.com, freep.com, metrotimes.com, sympathyrecords.com, chartattack.com, coversproject.com, golddollar.com, majesticdetroit.com, virtualfestivals.com, motorcityrocks.com, musiccomh.com, q4music.com, top40charts.com, italyrecords.com, dbetree.org, bpi.co.uk, damagedgoods.co.uk, mtv.com, villagevoice.co, theebillychildish.com, spin.com, filter-mag.com.*

I'd like to thank everyone at Plexus for their assistance and support; Paul Woods, Rebecca Martin, Louise Coe, Terence Porter and Sandra Wake. Thanks also to Adam Ryan and Yvette Haynes for providing vital assistance or materials. Special thanks to Donna Greene for her assistance, endurance and interference.

We would like to thank the following photographers and picture agencies for supplying photographs: Dennis Kleiman/Retna; Michael Ochs Archives/Redferns; Tabatha Fireman/ Redferns; Damien Maguire/All Action; Martin Philbey/Redferns; Doug Coombe/Retna; Lex Van Rossen/ Redferns; Ebet Roberts/Redferns; Stewart Isbell/Retna; All Action; Suzan/All Action; Statia Molewski/Retna; Robert Gauthier/Retna; Ali Smith/Retna; Eric McNatt/Retna; Jeff Davy/Retna; J. Scott Wyn/Retna; Branimis Kvartue/Zuma/ Corbis; Sara De Boer/Retna; Jeff Kowalsky/Zuma/Corbis; Scott Gries/Getty. Other images courtesy XL Recordings; Sympathy For The Record Industry; Italy Records; Sub Pop Records; *NME*; *Mojo* and *Q* magazine.

It has not been possible in all cases to trace the copyright sources, and the publishers would be glad to hear from any such unacknowledged copyright holders.

Dick Porter